BEING CATHOLIC

BY RODGER VAN ALLEN / FOREWORD BY LAWRENCE S. CUNNINGHAM

BEING CATHOLIC

COMMONWEAL

FROM THE SEVENTIES TO THE NINETIES

A Campion Book

Loyola University Press
Chicago

Loyola University Press
3441 North Ashland Avenue
Chicago, Illinois 60657

Cover and interior design by Nancy Gruenke

Library of Congress Cataloging-in-Publication Data
Van Allen, Rodger.
  Being Catholic: Commonweal from the seventies to the nineties/
Rodger Van Allen; foreword by Lawrence S. Cunningham.
     p. cm.
  Includes bibliographical references and index.
  ISBN 0-8294-0744-8
  1. Commonweal (New York, N.Y.) 2. Catholic Church—United
States—History—20th century. 3. United States—Church history—
20th century. I. Title.
PN4900.C64V29 1993
051—dc20   92-40701
                                                 CIP

In grateful thanks
for the love, the faith, and the example
of my parents,
John F. and Helen T. Van Allen

Contents

Foreword

The publication of Rodger Van Allen's *The Commonweal and American Catholicism* (Fortress, 1974) coincided with the fiftieth anniversary of the founding of that journal. Van Allen's study, originally a doctoral dissertation, chronicled the maturation of *Commonweal* from its earliest beginnings through the tumultuous decades in which the journal had to take into account everything from the anti-Catholicism of the 1928 presidential race to the meaning of the revolution unleashed by the events of Vatican II. It also had to do this while sharpening its own understanding of what it meant to be a journal edited by lay people in a decidedly clerical church and what it meant to be Catholic when the operative ecclesiastical word was the adjective *Roman* rather than the noun *Catholic*.

Looking at Van Allen's chronicle of that first fifty years with the wisdom that hindsight provides leads to only one sure conclusion: we have come a long, long way. It was, after all, a magazine that bucked the tide on both Franco and Joe McCarthy just as it defended social justice, racial equality, and church reform at a time when such was a minority point of view.

Rereading Van Allen's first volume recently had the further effect of reminding me, as a fairly regular contributor to the journal, of the distinguished company that I have kept.

All the past Catholic grandees are there (G. K. Chesterton, Hilaire Belloc, Etienne Gilson, Jacques Maritain, Dorothy Day, Thomas Merton) as well as a number of other regular contributors, editors, and critics who later went on to make their names in other arenas (John Simon, William Pfaff, Wilfred Sheed, John Leo, Daniel Callahan, Peter Steinfels).

These writers, and others like them, created over the decades the hypothetical person, not always loved (because the term is used now and anon with a sneer), referred to as the *Commonweal* Catholic. At one time *Commonweal* Catholics were probably easy to characterize. They read Gilson and Maritain; they wanted a vernacular liturgy; they had their doubts about the Blue Army and were mostly Democrats; they opposed racial segregation and, finally, they did not think that reading Graham Greene was an occasion of sin. They were, in short, every authoritarian pastor's worst nightmare.

Van Allen's first volume ended its chronicle in the year 1974. By that time whatever euphoria had been created by Vatican II was fast being dissipated as reality set in and the full impact of *Humanae Vitae* and the tumultuous social and political events of 1968 and its aftermath took their toll on the liberal psyche. What was the post-1968 *Commonweal* Catholic beyond that of the stereotypical one lampooned years later by Andrew Greeley in 1980 as "waspish, shrill, strident, and negative"? Some, like Michael Novak, hung up their Nehru jackets for a more "buttoned-down" neo-conservative look while others, like Daniel Callahan, simply jumped ship. The story, in short, gets complicated, and it is the burden of this present volume to uncomplicate it well enough to tell a coherent story. It does that admirably.

What strikes one the most when reading these pages is how so many public issues in the United States get enmeshed together with inescapably religious ones: the abortion issue (which takes up so much space in the magazine) can only be read in tandem with Van Allen's story of *Commonweal's* reflection on the American presidency since some Catholics linked the two points in such a way that thorny questions of hierarchical authority, individual conscience, the foundations of morality, and the obligations of the Christian in and to the commonweal become inevitable. For all of the messiness— and, at times, ruthlessness of these debates—they do highlight very important issues. As much as one may wish to disagree with the position that *Commonweal* has taken on any specific question, nobody, in all fairness it seems to me, could accuse the magazine of failing to take seriously a Christian response to the challenges provided by a secular and—more importantly—pluralist society.

A journal of opinion like *Commonweal* must, of necessity, be a political journal but unlike, say the *Nation* or the *New Republic,* it is also, unabashedly, a magazine written from a Catholic Christian perspective. It is interesting to note how hospitable the pages of *Commonweal* have been to a wide range of American Catholic intellectuals. If one—just to cite a conspicuous example—thinks of Catholic women, one need only look at the work of such professional writers as Mary Gordon and Barbara Grizzuti Harrison or such theologians as Lisa Cahill, Mary Durkin, Monika K. Hellwig, and Anne Patrick as well as activist Catholics from columnist Abigail McCarthy to one-time staffer Karen Sue Smith, who currently edits *Church.*

That same passion for the Christian angle resulted over the past decade in some memorable controversies over matters about which Catholics quite rightly feel passionate. The James Burtchaell/Daniel Maguire debate over abortion produced the longest articles ever published in the pages of the magazine. The exchange between then editor Peter Steinfels with former *Commonweal* regular Michael Novak and, later, with George Weigel was a classic *mano a mano* between liberals and neo-conservatives. Equally peppery were the exchanges provoked by articles such as that of Richard McBrien on homosexuality and the priesthood and by Margaret O'Brien Steinfels's more recent pleas for a bit more civility and less posturing in church debate.

But let me stop. It is unseemly to list all of the persons and events that Van Allen chronicles in this narrative. What was noted in the above paragraphs was not done so in order to say "*Commonweal* is important" but rather as a way of saying (to myself?) that these were great intellectual treats when first encountered on the journal's pages, and it is pleasant to savor them again.

It is that sense of anticipation that most pleases me when my *Commonweal* arrives; the anticipation that my mind will be nourished and my faith edified (from *aedificare*—to build up) and, perhaps, my prose style improved. Longtime readers of the journal will find this chronicle of its last two decades an exercise of recognition while those unfamiliar with its pages may be tempted to get acquainted. Beyond that, there is the more general contribution that Van Allen makes to the ongoing history of American Catholic culture. For all those reasons, he is to be saluted for a job well done.

Lawrence S. Cunningham
Department of Theology
University of Notre Dame

Acknowledgments

I am grateful to Leonard Swidler of Temple University who has been a most generous and wise professor, mentor, advisor, and friend through many years. It was he who suggested to me the contribution that the study of *Commonweal* could make, and thus both *The Commonweal and American Catholicism* (Fortress, 1974) and this volume owe their inspiration ultimately to him. Neither book would have been possible, however, without the full cooperation that was extended to me by *Commonweal* editors past and present. Edward S. Skillin, Peter Steinfels, James O'Gara, and Margaret O'Brien Steinfels were particularly generous in the time they granted me for taped interviews and follow-up correspondence.

I am delighted that since the publication of the earlier book, *Commonweal's* files are now in the very professional care of the Archives of the Hesburgh Library of the University of Notre Dame, where Charles Lamb has given them his capable attention. I am grateful to the Cushwa Center for the Study of American Catholicism at Notre Dame and its director, Jay P. Dolan, for facilitating my access to those files by a Travel and Research Grant and to all those at Notre Dame who assisted in various ways with my work and stay at Notre Dame. In addition to Professor Dolan, these include Jaime Vidal, Philip Gleason, Ralph McInerney, John Cavadini, Reverend Thomas K. Zurcher, C.S.C., and Lawrence Cunningham.

I am particularly grateful to Professor Cunningham, Chair of the Theology Department at Notre Dame, for the writing of the foreword to this book and for the dialogue with him regarding the book's title. Originally entitled *Toward the Creative Inculturation of Catholicism in America: Commonweal from the Seventies to the Nineties,* it evolved to simply *Being Catholic,* with the same subtitle.

The staffs of the library of St. Charles Borromeo Seminary and Villanova University have been most helpful in this project, and consistent support for my research from Villanova including a Faculty Research Grant has been deeply appreciated. Reverend Francis A. Eigo, O.S.A., and Emily Binns have been supportive in their roles as successive chairs for the Religious Studies Department. The departmental office staff members Roseann Ahern, Darla Krikorian, and Barbara Romano have helped in many ways. My graduate assistants, Cathy Graham Johnson and Margaret Fogarty, have been simply wonderful.

I am honored to have this manuscript published by Loyola University Press. Loyola University of Chicago can be rightly proud of its alumni who have played such a major role in *Commonweal*. John Cogley was the first to arrive at *Commonweal* from Loyola. James O'Gara followed not long after, with Peter Steinfels and Margaret O'Brien Steinfels after that. For the past quarter century the editor of *Commonweal* has been a graduate of Loyola. I find it particularly fitting, therefore, to have this work come forth from Loyola University Press, whose commitment to Catholic scholarship is long established. It has been a pleasure to work with the Reverend Joseph F. Downey, S.J., editorial director of the Press and associate editor June Sawyers. The distinguished artist and designer Emil Antonucci has graciously assisted in preparing his *Commonweal* covers for reproduction in the text. The credit for the photo of Edward S. Skillin goes to Sister Martha Mary McGaw, C.S.J., of *The Sooner Catholic*.

Finally, my thanks to my wife, Judy, and our family, Rodger, Katie, Tom and Dott, Paul, and Peter, who continue to be a great source of inspiration and good humor.

Commonweal Staff: 1973–1993

* Edward S. Skillin	Editorial Staff	1933–1938
	Coeditor	1938–1947
	Editor	1947–1967
	Publisher	1967–present
James O'Gara	Managing Editor	1952–1967
	Editor	1967–1978
Peter Steinfels	Editorial Assistant	1964–1965
	Assistant Editor	1965–1967
	Associate Editor	1967–1972
	Executive Editor	1978–1984
	Editor	1984–1988
John Fandel	Poetry Editor	1964–1979
Anne Robertson	Editorial Assistant	1965–1984
	Production Editor	1984–1989
John Deedy	Managing Editor	1967–1978
Raymond Schroth	Assistant Editor	1972–1973
	Associate Editor	1973–1979
Daniel M. Murtaugh	Assistant Editor	1979–1980
David Toolan	Assistant Editor	1979–1987
	Associate Editor	1987–1989
* Rosemary Deen	Poetry Coeditor	1979–1985
	Poetry Editor	1985–present
Marie Ponsot	Poetry Coeditor	1979–1985
* Patrick Jordan	Assistant Editor	1984–1987
	Associate Editor	1987–1990
	Managing Editor	1990–present

Karen Sue Smith	Assistant Editor	1984–1987
	Associate Editor	1987–1990
* Margaret O'Brien Steinfels	Editor	1988–present
* Robert Hoyt	Senior Writer	1988–present
Patricia Mazzola	Production Editor	1989–1991
* Paul Baumann	Associate Editor	1990–present
* Jacqueline Dowdell	Production Editor	1991–present

Critics

* Gerald Weales	"The Stage"	1968–present
Colin L. Westerbeck, Jr.	"Movies"	1971–1984
Tom O'Brien	"Movies"	1984–1990
* Richard Alleva	"Movies"	1990-present

*Indicates current *Commonweal* staff

Introduction

The lay-edited Catholic journal *Commonweal* has long been recognized as occupying an important place in the life and thought of the Catholic community in the United States. The infrequently used word *commonweal,* meaning the common well-being or general welfare, was chosen as the title of the magazine because it was most indicative of the spirit and purpose of *Commonweal,* which was never intended to be read only by Catholics nor to serve some merely introspective end. The origins of the journal began in 1922 with a group of Ivy League and relatively affluent Catholics who wanted a journal "as highbrow as the *New Republic*" that would be "expressive of the Catholic note" in literature, the arts, and the discussion of economic and social topics. George Shuster, who joined the magazine shortly after its beginning, has recalled that "very few people objected to *The Commonweal* in those days in terms of doctrine or even in terms of being a lay organ, but they detested the notion that we were going to be highbrow."[1]

Commonweal's writing style has been one of a graceful and polished simplicity rather than stuffy or pretentious. Further, the magazine's commitment to clear communication to an educated and concerned readership has resulted in *Commonweal's* being regarded as the most broadly intellectual of Catholic publications. Father Theodore M. Hesburgh, C.S.C., Notre Dame's president from the early 1950s to the late 1980s, describes *Commonweal* as "loyal to its Catholic tradition—and free to question it, reassess it, keep it alive, put it to work on current questions." This makes *Commonweal,* says Hesburgh, "a uniquely useful resource."[2] In 1964, when Father Andrew M. Greeley and Peter H. Rossi wanted to survey what they called the Catholic "liberal intelligentsia" for their study *The Education of Catholic Americans,* they used a randomly selected sample of one thousand *Commonweal* readers.[3]

From its first issue in 1924, *Commonweal* has been conscious of speaking not only to Catholics but to other readers as well, and this was one factor in bringing respect and attention to the thoughts it expressed. For example, when a 1928 papal encyclical on ecumenism was published, *The Congregationalist* magazine stated that they "should like to know what such excellent and intelligent Roman Catholic laymen as, for instance, those who conduct *The Commonweal*, really think of this business (the pope's encyclical)."[4] Respect for *Commonweal* as an independent and intelligent vehicle of Catholic thought has resulted in its presence in most community libraries and virtually all academic libraries. Its total circulation throughout the 1970s and 1980s remained about 18,000, a number comparable to other such intellectual journals. Its significance, clearly, is found not in any massive circulation but in its tradition of excellence.

One conclusion reached in *The Commonweal and American Catholicism,* a study of *Commonweal's* first fifty years, was that the magazine had recapitulated in its history the broad outline of the history of Catholics in the United States. To put it briefly, both were dramas in three acts, with long second acts. Each followed an evolution from what might in one sense be called patrician origins through immigrant-Catholic coming of age to maturity and identity crisis. That evolution brought both the story of the magazine and the story of Catholics in the United States to the early 1970s.

But what might now be said for the magazine since that time, and perhaps, indirectly, for Catholics in the United States since that time? The pursuit of this question is the purpose of what follows as we attempt to focus on some of the notable and instructive issues and events in the pages of *Commonweal* during those years. We will also look, to some degree, behind the scenes into the context and thinking of the editors responsible for *Commonweal.*

As we begin our consideration in the 1970s, we will neglect such subjects as the Vietnam War, the 1972 presidential election, and President Richard M. Nixon and Watergate, all of which were treated in our earlier study. At *Commonweal,* at this particular time, we find that James O'Gara, a Catholic layman from Chicago and a veteran of both the Catholic Worker movement and World War II, is the editor. When he assumed that post in 1967 after fifteen years as managing editor, he succeeded Edward Skillin, who then became publisher. John

Deedy, a very experienced Catholic journalist, editor, and
author, serves as managing editor, a post he has held since
1967. Raymond A. Schroth, a Jesuit priest who became the
first cleric to serve as an editor in 1972, is the associate editor.
Anne Robertson, at *Commonweal* since 1960, is editorial assistant (later production editor). These five people form the
entire full-time editorial staff who, at 232 Madison Avenue in
New York, occupy an office where the marginal economics of
the magazine have dictated an office style that would make it
serve as a suitable set for *The Front Page,* the 1920s drama-
comedy. The address is rather fancy and is located in the publishing district. The atmosphere can be described as cheerful
people in a rather gray setting. A necessary and unresisted
simplicity of style doesn't quite explain the downright ascetic
approach to painting the place, but the pressure of producing
a weekly magazine with such a small staff might explain such
inattention.

Enough has been said by way of scene-setting. Let us turn
to some of the important issues, beginning with the abortion
question that has been such a significant concern from the
1970s into the 1990s.

1

Abortion

Commonweal acknowledged that in some states abortion laws that were too restrictive needed reform and that it had been argued well that abortion should be allowed as a lesser evil in special cases "when the mother's life is endangered, rape, incest or a severely damaged fetus," but the magazine was not pleased by the Supreme Court's sweeping *Roe v. Wade* decision of January 22, 1973. "What a society values," it argued, "it protects with laws." State laws restricting abortion "testified to some consensus that life in process *is life* and must be protected. Now, says the Court, that consensus is gone." The Court had "diminished the whole concept of what it means to be a person, and had succumbed to that cultural elitism that marks cultures content with their values while slipping into decline." The United States was, they felt, "in danger of becoming an abortion culture—one which cringes from the thought of death yet sanctions real death and living death for the convenience of the ruling class." They saw an abortion culture built on an individualism that affirmed "the rights of the strongest individuals to thrive" and a "privacy" that was "not primarily a protection of the person but a system of isolation—withdrawal from the full implications and responsibilities of sex and love." Such a culture offers "a comfortable way of life that settles for the least inconvenient solution to moral dilemmas—like bombing." This last comment, a reference to the experience in Vietnam, was more obvious then than now.

In facing the future after the Court's decision, *Commonweal* forecast:

> If the abortion debate continues on the present—women's exclusive right-to-decide vs. "It's murder"—level, and if the public continues to view abortion in isolation from other social and moral problems, the anti-abortion cause will become the political tool of the right wing, of those who would resolve complex political problems with instant constitutional amendments and theological debates by excommunicating their opponents, of those who have consistently backed a murderous war, opposed gun control, and fought labor, health and welfare legislation designed to enhance the dignity of society's weakest members.

The editors found the "official" church response to the decision "an embarrassment—episcopal fulminations and full-page dead-fetus pictures in the diocesan press." The bishops had "lost their credibility on sexual morality by their dogmatic opposition to birth control; and few can take them seriously as guardians of human life when they can preach homilies at the White House and not speak for the innocent children of Vietnam killed by our bombs and shells." The editorial concluded with the following paragraph:

> What should the church do now? Radically re-educate itself on both the value of *every* human life and its own need to take a less compliant and more prophetic stance against the trend toward egoism and selfishness in our government, culture and church. Support responsible birth control so people will learn to decide about a child before it is conceived. Take women seriously and give them real status in the community of the church so that

childbearing is not seen just as a woman's joy-burden but as a community responsibility. Make it socially acceptable and financially possible to have a child outside of marriage. Really be pro-life: champion all those whose lives are still in process, whose future is still precarious, whose true potentials are still struggling to be born.[1]

The same issue presented an article on the Court's decision by Father Robert F. Drinan, S.J., the U.S. Representative from Massachusetts who had formerly been dean of the Boston College Law School. Drinan's reading of the fifty-one page opinion of Justice Blackmun's decision left him with "the impression that seven members of the Supreme Court who concurred in Blackmun's judgment came to the conclusion that abortion

should not be a crime and then searched for the least painful and least controversial way to justify their conclusion."[2] Drinan found the majority's argument from the right of privacy "astonishing." He pointed out dissenting Justice Rehnquist's opinion that the concept of privacy used in the case was "not even a 'distant cousin' to any notion of privacy hitherto acted upon by the Supreme Court." He also quoted Justice White's opinion that the Court was using "raw judicial power" and had "scarcely any reason or authority for its action." The Court, Drinan pointed out, had gone far beyond the limited liberalization recommended by the prestigious American Law Institute, the American Medical Association, and the American Bar Association.

The Debate Continues in the Seventies

In 1974, Paul Ramsey, the distinguished Princeton ethics professor and a Methodist layman, argued in *Commonweal* for "an amendment to the Constitution that would return to the states their legislative power to protect the unborn child from privatized physician-patient decisions about its life or death."³ Ramsey pointed out that this would not bind the decisions that the states might make. He did feel that the states would show some appreciation of the "factual evidence . . . for the individuated humanity of the unborn child." Citing Paul Freund, an expert in constitutional law, that our system of division of powers—executive, legislative, and judicial—ultimately rested on constitutional morality, Ramsey in the context of Nixon's Watergate affair, argued that just as impeachment procedures might be employed against an imperial presidency that exceeded its powers, so also a constitutional amendment returning the abortion issue to the states might be used "to correct a decision of an imperial Court." Ramsey did not argue for a constitutional amendment protecting the unborn. Neither did Daniel A. Degnan, a Jesuit priest and professor at Syracuse University Law School. Like Ramsey, Degnan favored a constitutional amendment returning to the states the power to prohibit abortions. Degnan specifically added his hope for "a common position, shared by as many Americans as possible, in laws which would allow for some abortions, but which would attempt to restrict the taking of fetal life in both the middle and later months of pregnancy."⁴

In an editorial in the same issue, *Commonweal* supported the approach outlined by Degnan. The magazine favored working for a consensus that would oppose wholesale abortion, while permitting it in hardship cases such as rape, incest, or a fetus with severe birth defects. The key people to be addressed were "moderate-minded, middle-of-the-road Americans who favor abortion in hardship cases but who are not firmly committed on the question of large-scale abortion— a group, Catholics should remember, which includes both Jews of various theological outlooks and committed Christians of other denominations who believe that abortion, like war, can be justified under certain circumstances." Because of the necessity to cooperate with others, Catholic leaders should "abandon their vain hopes for any kind of total legal ban on abortion." Such an absolute ban would be "impossible as well as ill advised." Working together, however, it would be possible for Catholics and others opposed to wholesale abortion to map a prudent course that "would permit abortion only for serious cause, while at the same time supplying full and effective help for women who are willing to have their babies."[5]

Thus *Commonweal* took a moderate position regarding abortion and the law. There was, the magazine stated, a distinction between civil law and morality. The law could not and should not ban everything considered immoral. Abortion should not be absolutely prohibited, but neither should it be absolutely permitted. The editors were appalled by the statistics that cited "over half a million legal abortions in one 30 month period in New York City alone."[6] *Commonweal*'s perception that there was a creative and responsible middle majority position on abortion was remarkably on target. In a statistical pattern, constant since 1973, we find that only one American in five favors a completely permissive approach to abortion, and only one in five favors a completely prohibitive approach. The profile is the same for Catholics and for other Americans and does not vary significantly from region to region.[7] Over the years, however, little has been done to mobilize this middle majority that favors permitting abortions only in some circumstances. That is, the group has been ignored by a media that find it easier and more dramatic to highlight minority views that flank it on either side.

In 1975, *Commonweal* ran a forum-style debate entitled "The Abortion Decision: Two Years Later" between two authors who were professors at the Loyola University School of Law in Los Angeles. Raymond G. Decker focused on the Court's respect for the conscience of the mother and found the decision "more Christian than its critics." Walter R. Trinkaus, however, said that "the existing living victim" of abortion was the crucial consideration, and he likened the case to the Court's infamous antebellum Dred Scott case.[8]

In 1977, the U.S. Supreme Court ruled that neither the U.S. Constitution nor federal Medicaid legislation required states to pay for abortions. This, plus moves within both the Department of Health, Education, and Welfare and the Congress to cut off federal funds for abortion, "put the brakes on the rush to abortion as if it were a morally indifferent alternative to birth control," said *Commonweal*. It also provided an opportunity to work toward "a national family policy that would embody the values of both religious and secular

humanism." They praised President Jimmy Carter and HEW
Secretary Joseph Califano for their plan to subsidize the adop-
tion of children and challenged Catholic leaders to lobby for
support programs that would enhance positive alternatives to
abortion. They "should not automatically oppose a candidate
who wants to use city or state funds for abortion when his
other social policies might make abortions less desirable." On
dissenting Justice Blackmun's claim that as a result of the
majority decision "the cancer of poverty will continue to
grow," they said he missed the point.

> Abortion doesn't cure poverty. It kills the unborn
> children of the poor. The far deeper scandal is the
> disgusting inequitable distribution of wealth and
> public services in our society, where the poor are
> terrified to bring children into the world for fear that
> they cannot grow and prosper, marry happily, and
> have children and grandchildren of their own.
> Abortion can easily be a rich person's solution to a
> poor family's problem—one that spares the upper
> classes the burden of facing the social unrest gener-
> ated by a multiplying poor, black populace.[9]

Writing in the same issue, columnist Peter Steinfels, who
would join the staff of *Commonweal* full time and become its
executive editor in 1978, challenged a *New York Times* editorial that called the restriction of federal funds for abortion "out-
rageous." For Steinfels, the policy respected the rights of the
poor and others in the privacy argument in *Roe v. Wade* and
yet refused abortion acceptance as social policy: "If the moral
status of the fetus is too unsettled for purposes of restricting
abortion, then it is also too unsettled for purposes of publicly
paying for abortion." Referring to teenage pregnancies and
other high-risk births, the *Times* had asked, "Will the anti-
abortion forces that have carried the day now form an effective political coalition to insure humane conditions of life for
these children and their parents?" Steinfels found the question
a fair one. He granted that opponents of abortion would be
most persuasive on the basis of their generosity to those in
need. He felt, however, that the argument cut both ways:

Have those without moral objections to abortion seriously considered any other alternative for these women except public funding? . . . Could those earning their livelihood from abortion contribute services? Could a private fund feed and clothe them, send them to school, watch them be raised? The *Times* suggests that until those opposed to abortion come to the aid of the poor, "the humanity of their movement will remain in doubt." What about the humanity of the movement supporting abortion? Is it unequivocally demonstrated merely by a demand for public money?

Steinfels regretted that the politics of abortion had always been "intensely emotional and narrow, with neither philosophical issues nor the public interest receiving much careful attention."[10]

In 1978, the Hyde Amendment—the congressional rider on HEW's budget that restricted Medicaid reimbursements for abortion to a very limited range of cases—was challenged by a class action suit, *McRae v. Califano.* Among the plaintiffs challenging the amendment was the Women's Division of the Board of Global Ministries of the United Methodist Church, and among the plaintiffs' representatives were attorneys from Planned Parenthood and the American Civil Liberties Union.

The plaintiffs maintained that the Hyde Amendment was equivalent to the establishment of a religion—Roman Catholicism in particular but also of other religious viewpoints that were opposed to abortion, including Orthodox Jewish, Mormon, and various Lutheran, Methodist, and Baptist positions. The congressional action, they argued, had no other basis than a sectarian theological one. It had no proper secular purpose, advanced one religious viewpoint at the expense of another, and involved excessive government entanglement with religion.

Commonweal argued that neither the religious roots of a public policy, the language and beliefs of its supporters, nor the central motives of the policymakers were central to disqualifying that policy as without a legitimate secular purpose. The editors quoted Lawrence Tribe from *American*

Constitutional Law: "If a purpose were to be classified as non-secular simply because it coincided with the beliefs of one religion or took its origin from another, virtually nothing the government does would be acceptable; laws against murder, for example, would be forbidden because they overlapped the fifth commandment of the Mosaic Decalogue." One simply did not know precisely what were the grounds on which the representatives and senators supporting the Hyde amendment reached their decision. "It is quite possible, indeed quite likely, that many who are not opposed to abortion itself are nonetheless opposed to *government funding* of abortion—the real issue at hand—because of a political attitude about government's role in morally controverted issues or a pragmatic belief about compromise in a pluralistic society." *Commonweal* felt that whatever the mixture of beliefs behind it, Congress's decision to protect fetal life was "as secular on the face of it as its decisions to protect tracts of wilderness from spoilation, unknowing consumers from toxic drugs, or laboratory animals from cruel experimentation." They also found providing taxpayers' funds for some purpose far more "entangling" than simply withdrawing from the area altogether.

The editorial entitled "Do Catholics Have Constitutional Rights?" maintained that the reasoning of the plaintiffs amounted to "the disenfranchisement of American Catholics of their rights to political activity." The plaintiffs presented a Catch-22 situation: Catholics, they said, were free to picket, to lobby, and to enter into any pastoral or political activities; if anything resulted from these activities, however, it should be declared unconstitutional on the basis that it was Catholic picketing and lobbying that produced the results! This reasoning not only disenfranchised Catholics from active engagement in the political process; logically, it disenfranchised all religious viewpoints. The argument would seem to apply also to Jewish mobilization on behalf of Israel, to the broad mobilization in the religious community for civil rights legislation, and to the nineteenth-century agitation by religious abolitionists.

The *Commonweal* editors noted that the plaintiffs in *McRae* cited *Commonweal* at several points, with quotes from editorials and articles that complained of the narrowness of vision or untoward tactics of the right-to-life effort. The editors then asked that the plaintiffs "take to heart our equal distress at their own vision and tactics." The editorial concluded:

> Not long ago we received a plaintive letter asking support for the American Civil Liberties Union. The ACLU was trying to make clear that its defense of Nazis in the notorious Skokie case arose from its belief that the ACLU action protected the First Amendment rights of all citizens. We sympathize with the ACLU's plight in communicating its motives. But we do wonder, first, at the religious groups like the Methodist Women who undermine their own political rights in order to win an immediate victory and, second, at the ACLU attorneys who cannot be at least as solicitous of the First Amendment when a controversy involves American Catholics as when it involves American Nazis.[11]

The editorial opened up an interesting dialogue that included, in opposition, a reply editorial by Aryeh Neier in *The Nation* and lengthy correspondence from the Counsel to the Reproductive Freedom, American Civil Liberties Project, and others at the ACLU and Planned Parenthood as well as the associate general secretary for the Methodist Board of Global Ministries and attorney Leo Pfeffer; in agreement, an editorial in the *Wall Street Journal* entitled "A New Anti-Catholic Bigotry?" and letters from Lutheran pastor Richard Neuhaus, the senior editor of *Worldview,* and Illinois Rep. Henry J. Hyde.[12]

Pro-choice advocates at the ACLU, having noted *Commonweal's* editorials criticizing aspects of the activities of the pro-life forces seemed surprised when *Commonweal* took a critical stance on aspects of their own activities. Secure in their own vision of progressive wisdom, the ACLU stated: "Just as today's opposition to anti-abortion laws draws accusations of anti-Catholicism, so in the 1920s opponents of the 'monkey' laws were labeled 'anti-Christian.'" They felt that "anti-choice Catholics, like Mormons, Orthodox Jews or fundamentalist Protestants who support the present campaign to restrict abortion . . . have no . . . right to enact their religious beliefs in law."[13]

In a four-page editorial *Commonweal* argued that there was no evidence to substantiate the theme that ran throughout the critical correspondence and the plaintiff's case, namely that a narrow or particular theology was being "imposed" on the mass of citizens. The editors pointed out that the Gallup poll indicated that only 35 percent of Americans favored providing abortions at government expense and that of the large and diverse group of Americans opposed to government funding, there was no evidence that they were motivated by theological doctrines and certainly no evidence that they were motivated "exclusively" by theological doctrines as Aryeh Neier had argued.

The editorial continued *Commonweal*'s critical dialogue with both pro-life and pro-choice forces. Concerning the former it said: "The recent action of the National Right to Life Committee in choosing a 1980 'hit list' consisting almost entirely of liberal Congressmen . . . raises the question of whether 'right to life' will become nothing more than 'life to the right,' a manipulative adjunct to the new right-wing politics." Concerning the latter, it said pro-choice forces made little effort to understand abortion opponents, "writing them off as 'absolutist,' a curious adjective one never finds applied to those who will brook no anti-Semitism, no sexual inequality, or no corporate bribery." The left, it said, repeatedly insists that those opposed to abortion are free to have them or not, which is to miss the whole point of conflict, namely the belief of such opponents that the life of another party is at stake. *Commonweal* summarized its view by saying that its "real complaint against the plaintiffs in *McRae*, then, is essentially our complaint about the bishops and so many right-to-lifers. In their single-mindedness about one concern, they are running rough-shod over numerous other values to which they owe responsibility."[14] On June 30, 1980, the Supreme Court held that limiting Medicaid funding of abortion did not work an impermissible establishment of religion and did not involve excessive government entanglement with religion.[15]

The Debate Continues in the Eighties

In November 1981, *Commonweal* devoted a special issue to the abortion topic, earning a first-place award from the Catholic Press Association. The judges commended the magazine for an outstanding job that explored the whole abortion issue without screaming. *Commonweal's* editorial emphasized that though many were "bone-weary of the subject," one could not afford to indulge this fatigue. It required authentic moral judgment and a commitment to "seeking the common good as a pluralistic society." The editors warned against evading the issue by either shunning it altogether or by single-mindedly concentrating on only one aspect of it while ignoring all the complicating realities.

> Denouncing the inconsistencies of one or both sides of activists, resigning oneself to whatever the Supreme Court has decided, reducing the question to one of "choice" abstracted from the problem of what is being chosen, feeling the tragedy of the fetus but not of the mother, insisting on the rights of the women who are born but not on any rights for the unborn, whether female or male, pretending that abortion is opposed by only a small group of Americans, pretending that abortion is sought or defended only by selfish individuals—these are all ways of evading the burden of authentic moral judgment.[16]

The lead article was from the then forthcoming book *The Politics of Abortion: A Study of Community Conflict in Public Policy-Making* by Raymond Tatalovich and Byron W. Daynes, which traced the issue from the 1959 origin of the movement for abortion reform through the 1969–1973 drive for abortion repeal to the current level of conflict and some consensus, which, as the authors saw it, was essentially abortion reform: yes; abortion repeal: no.

This meant a legally permissive attitude toward hardcase abortion situations of rape, incest, or threat to the life of the mother but did not mean a general approval of abortion. They concluded that the major lesson to be learned from abortion politics "unfortunately, is that we had to experience the debilitating effects of this long struggle in order to fashion a solution to the abortion issue which was so obviously indicated two decades ago—before the intrusion of the Supreme Court." Mary Meehan, a self-described ex-Catholic, in "Catholic Liberals and Abortion: Time to Move Beyond Agonizing,"[17] argued that "it is biology not faith, that tells us that a fertilized ovum is the earliest form of human life." She said that Catholic-baiting by the National Abortion Rights Action League started long ago and that it was in fact a conscious policy of NARAL founder Lawrence Lader. She documented her case by quoting Dr. Bernard Nathanson's report in *Aborting America* on Lader's strategy session with Nathanson when the two were close colleagues in NARAL. Lader told Nathanson: "Historically every revolution has to have its villain. It doesn't really matter whether it's a king, a dictator, or a tsar, but it has to be *someone*." Lader made it clear to Nathanson that he had in mind a special group of people:

> Not just all Catholics. First of all that's too large a group, and for us to vilify them all would diffuse our focus. Secondly, we have to convince liberal Catholics to join us, a popular front as it were, and if we tar them all with the same brush, we'll just antagonize a few who might otherwise have joined us and be valuable showpieces for us. No, it's got to be the Catholic *hierarchy*.[18]

In the context of the contraception dispute, attacks on the Catholic hierarchy by NARAL, Meehan said, instead of antagonizing the liberal laity, may really have attracted them to the NARAL view. She advised liberals—by and large, conservatives supported contraception teaching—who might encounter sneering references to pro-lifers as "so-called right-to-lifers" or "friends of the fetus" to remember that segregationists in the 1950s used the charge of being a "nigger lover" in their effort to dehumanize both black people and white civil rights activists. She said she understood the social pressure on liberals to march to the steady pro-choice drumbeat of liberal publications like the *Nation,* the *New Republic,* the *New York*

Times, and others but urged that they not be liberals "of the knee-jerk variety" and that they "question the infallibility of the ACLU and the Democratic party at least as much as you question the infallibility of the pope."[19]

In his article, "Beyond the Stereotypes," sociologist James R. Kelly reported on his in-depth study of pioneer right-to-life activists. Kelly's three-hour interviews with twenty-eight activists, consisting of fourteen women and fourteen men, yielded results that indicated a movement with originators far different from the sectarian, morally naive, and politically conservative people envisioned in the liberal-left stereotype. Most were what Kelly called "economic liberals" and more than one-quarter had "personal experience with extremely vulnerable forms of human life," retarded children, and senile or handicapped parents, whom they felt were implicitly devalued by legalized abortion and its underlying principle.[20]

Executive editor Peter Steinfels contributed an important article to the special issue on abortion. "The Search for an Alternative: Can Liberal Catholicism Make a Distinct Contribution?" argued that it indeed could. Steinfels proposed two steps. First, give up the idea entertained by some that the abortion issue can be resolved without legislative restriction on abortion. "What merit there is in these schemes rests on the hope that psychological or social incentives can allow cultural disapprobation of abortion to coexist with a completely noncoercive legal treatment of it." Steinfels felt it was "sociological fantasy" to believe that society could effectively insist on the value of fetal life while refusing to restrict legislatively any assault that a woman might choose on the value. This first step required liberal Catholics to disagree frankly with the pro-choice forces. His second step required them to do the same with the pro-life movement. "Just as the pro-choice movement seems utterly oblivious to biology in discussing (when it does) the issue of 'humanhood,' the right-to-life movement is naively overconfident in its belief that the existence of a unique 'genetic package' from conception onward settles the abortion issue." Steinfels continued: "Yes, it does prove that what is involved is a human individual and not 'part of the mother's body.' It does not prove that, say, a twenty-eight-day-old embryo, approximately the size of this parenthesis (-), is *then and there* a creature with the same claims to preservation and protection as a newborn or an adult." While not dismissing the appeal to the potentiality of the embryo as false, Steinfels argued for a goal of prohibiting abortion after eight weeks of development. "At this point, when the embryo is now termed a fetus, all organs are present that will later be developed fully, the heart has been pumping for a month; the unborn individual has a distinctive human appearance, responds to stimulation of its nose or mouth, and is over an inch in size. Electrical activity in its brain is now discernible." He didn't say that this was the "magic moment" when "human life begins." Rather, it was "one moment when an accumulation of evidence should compel a majority, even in a pluralist society and despite whatever obscurities about early life continue to be debated, to agree that the unborn individual now deserves legal protection." After this point, abortion should be permitted only for the most serious of reasons, he concluded. Such should be the minimum national policy, "established if necessary by constitutional amendment."

What would such a prohibition accomplish in practice? Steinfels granted that it would prevent fewer than half of current abortions, but it "would be a decisive step back from *Roe v. Wade*" and "would be a statement about the seriousness and moral precariousness of abortion at any stage." It was clear that advocates of this position were not relying on any church's moral code and that they represented a reasonable compromise. Steinfels concluded: "We cannot rest with the two alternatives of *Roe v. Wade* or a ban on all abortion from the time of conception: the former is morally intolerable; the latter, politically and socially impossible. Liberal Catholics cannot let the present dominance of those alternatives be an excuse for abdication." There was no evident reaction, however, to this searching and serious article by Peter Steinfels.[21]

In 1983, two years after the Steinfels article and ten years after *Roe v. Wade*, an important *Commonweal* editorial presented a concise summary:

> It would be comforting to have a solution, complete and neatly packaged, to the abortion question. Sorry. For better or worse, this journal has pro-

ceeded negatively on this issue over the past decade. *Roe v. Wade*, we have argued, was a legal and moral disaster. So was the widespread resort to abortion that exploded in the wake of its legitimation by the Court. On the other hand, a human life amendment that bans all or virtually all, abortions is probably unachievable; in any case would be unenforceable; and if somehow politically engineered in the absence of a massive change in public opinion, would be swiftly reversed after doing fatal damage to the right-to-life cause.

Commonweal did not, however, suggest either a throwing up of one's hands in despair or a complacent settlement into "wiser-than-thou" neutrality. Instead, the editors suggested that the best way to arrive at a realistic position in the abortion dispute was to define what should be *avoided*. There are four things to avoid: (1) reducing the dispute to slogans; (2) making peace with abortion; (3) putting all one's hopes in the law or all one's energies into politics; and (4) avoidance itself. By avoidance itself the editors meant the avoiding, for convenience, of certain realities practiced by pro-life and pro-choice ranks. On the pro-life side, there was an avoidance of some real and terrible conflicts. "Not that every abortion involves a caring woman or couple trapped amidst multiple obligations; but far too many do for the fact to be brushed aside. It is one thing to believe that abortion cannot be the solution; it is another and self-deceiving thing to believe there really is no problem."²² The editors felt that the pro-choice movement and "the liberal community generally" avoided the reality of the fetus. "As we have said, the question of the moral status of the unborn individual is not simple, but ultimately the question must be decided on its own terms and not on the grounds of the burdens that one or another conclusion would have on others. Whether animals or slaves or trees or nations have rights depends, at least first of all, on something to do with *them*, not on whether recognizing such rights would impose a hardship on us." *Commonweal* said that the pro-choice and liberal community resolutely avoided this question and did almost anything to change the subject. The editorial concluded: "Can they succeed for another ten years?"²³

Commonweal continued to give significant attention to abortion throughout the 1980s. "Breaking Through the Stereotypes"[24] by Daniel and Sidney Callahan won the 1985 Catholic Press Association Award for Best Article. The opening paragraph by the husband-and-wife team included the following: "Ever since the topic of abortion became of interest to us in the 1960s, we have disagreed. Well over half of our thirty years of marriage have been marked (though rarely marred) by an ongoing argument. For all of that period, one of us (Daniel) has taken a pro-choice position and the other (Sidney) a pro-life position (to use somewhat reluctantly, the common labels)." The article reported on a project that "sought to see if we could provide some better insight into how individuals weigh and order their values when dealing with abortion." The authors convened ten women, equally drawn from the pro-choice and pro-life sides, who represented an important group, "those women who, though they differ, are willing to talk with those on the other side, willing to make the effort to empathize with those who hold opposing views, and willing to see if they can find some shared ground to keep their dialogue alive."[25] The article reported that the outcome of the project did indeed break many stereotypes:

> Too often it is assumed that a commitment to feminism entails a pro-choice position; but that is only one version of feminism, not necessarily its essence. Too often it is assumed that a commitment to the family as an enduring value entails a prohibition of abortion, but that does not follow either. Too often it is assumed that a pro-choice stand entails treating children as disposable goods, of value only if wanted. But that is too often a parody of the genuine affirmation of the value of children that can be a central part of a pro-choice position. Too often it is assumed that a society which values the rights of individuals must deny the value of community and thus any social restrictions on abortion choices; but in some renderings a denial of abortion can be a way of affirming rights.

In 1986, two contrasting articles brought depth and range to the abortion discussion in *Commonweal*. The articles, written independently, were published in successive issues and generated some lengthy published correspondence. Sidney Callahan's "Abortion and the Sexual Agenda: A Case for Pro-Life Feminism" critiqued feminist arguments for the morality and legality of abortion and argued that opposition to abortion was in keeping with an expanded and properly focused feminist vision. The modern feminist movement had "made a mistaken move" at a critical juncture. "Rightly rebelling against patriarchy, unequal education, restricted work opportunities, and women's downtrodden political status," feminists also rejected "the older feminine sexual ethic of love and fidelity." Instead, "amative, erotic, permissive sexuality (along with abortion rights) became symbolically identified with other struggles for social equality in education, work and politics." Callahan felt that an ironic situation had developed in which many pro-choice feminists preached their own double standard.

> In the world of work and career, women are urged to grow up, to display mature self-discipline and self-control; they are told to persevere in long-term commitments, to cope with unexpected obstacles by learning to tough out the inevitable sufferings and setbacks entailed in life and work. But this mature ethic of commitment and self-discipline, recommended as the only way to progress in the world of work and personal achievement, is discounted in the domain of sexuality.

Callahan asked pro-choice feminists to rethink what kind of gender model really served women's best interests. Another and different round of feminist consciousness-raising was needed. This time, "instead of humbly buying entrée by conforming to male lifestyles," women should demand that society accommodate to them so that they can combine, appropriately, childbearing, education, and careers.[26]

The other article was written by Joan C. Callahan (no relation to Sidney Callahan). Callahan argued that the reluctance of some politicians to support anti-abortion legislation, despite their personal opposition to abortion, was justified. Working from the framework of this legal-political question, to which we will return in a later section dealing with presidential campaigns, Callahan developed the case against admitting human fetuses into the category of full-fledged persons with full-fledged fundamental rights. In her article "The Fetus and Fundamental Rights: Public Policy Requires Compelling Reasons," Callahan maintained that she did not find the arguments for fetal rights sufficiently compelling, and thus she found the position of Catholic liberal Democrats such as Geraldine Ferraro and Mario Cuomo reasonable, even though their explanations were not sufficiently thorough for her taste.[27] Many correspondents replied to these two articles, including Governor Mario Cuomo of New York, who told Joan Callahan that she spoke several times of Catholic liberal Democrats "almost as though there were a political party in our country similar to the Christian Democrats of other countries. There isn't. And I don't think this type of categorization is any more helpful than it would be to call others 'Protestant conservative Republicans.' "[28]

The most extensive single debate on abortion appeared in *Commonweal* on November 20, 1987. Earlier that year, on February 9, the theology department at the University of Notre Dame sponsored a major debate on the subject. The two debaters, in what was referred to at Notre Dame as a "heavyweight bout," were James Tunstead Burtchaell, C.S.C., and Daniel C. Maguire. Father Burtchaell is a professor of theology at Notre Dame, a former provost of the university, and the author of *Rachel Weeping: The Case Against Abortion* and other books. Professor Maguire is a professor of theology at

Marquette University, a past president of the Society of Christian Ethics, author of several books on ethics, and an active critic of official Catholic teaching on abortion. The proposition Burtchaell and Maguire debated was "Recent developments and reflection provide authentic reasons to reconsider the virtually total Christian disapproval of abortion."

The debate covered twenty pages and formed the longest single "article" in the history of the magazine.[29] Thirteen pages presented the position papers, the responses to one another, and the concluding statements of the speakers. Some audience questions and responses were also included. *Commonweal* continued the discussion with an additional seven pages, consisting of an editorial comment that sifted through the arguments on each side, raised some questions that added more focus to the debate, and provided specific responses by both Maguire and Burtchaell. The editors' comment on the debate was "Two powerful minds have come charging toward one another from opposite directions—and then unexpectedly crossed paths without collision. They were it turns out, operating on entirely different tracks."[30] This was at least partly the case. Maguire's argument was essentially historical, pointing out that what is called the "clear and constant" teaching of the church as absolutely opposing abortion is, in fact, neither clear nor constant but shows the ambiguity and difficulty of dealing with conflict situations. Burtchaell's argument was, as he himself put it, essentially prophetic. In his reading of early Christianity, he interpreted the unborn to be among those "the Jesus people" were called to safeguard along with the enemy, the slave, the wife, and the infant. That the Christian tradition was imperfect at times in its insights to the full dimensions of these responsibilities was beside the point.

If the differing approaches meant that there was no collision in the debate, that did not mean, however, that the debate had no value. Even with occasional verbal jabs on both sides—that failed, perhaps, to meet the typical *Commonweal* standard of civility—the debate managed to be illuminating, worthwhile, and, in fact, unique. Despite the atmosphere, in some official Catholic circles, at least, that has shut down dialogue on abortion, both Notre Dame and *Commonweal* demonstrated that the Catholic tradition's respect for reason and communication is as much of service on the subject of abortion as it is on other matters and concerns. *Commonweal* readers joined the discussion with six pages of follow-up correspondence to the Maguire-Burtchaell debate.[31]

2

Presidential Politics

Only on two occasions—in 1952, with Adlai E. Stevenson, and in 1972, with George McGovern—has *Commonweal* formally endorsed a presidential candidate. In 1976, encouraged by Jimmy Carter's selection of Walter Mondale as his vice-presidential running mate,[1] *Commonweal* warmed to the candidacy of the nuclear engineer, peanut farmer, and Georgia governor who had moved with efficiency from long-shot candidate to Democratic nominee. A *Commonweal* editorial just before the election gave him their "tilt," a clear enough nod though not a formal endorsement. Carter, they felt, would arrive at the White House with few political debts and would be freer than any president in recent American history to pursue the reforms outlined in his campaign. They added that they would be less than candid if they did not say that part of their "tilt toward Carter is due to the alternative to his election." Gerald Ford and Robert Dole, they felt, represented vested interests.[2] Earlier they had pointed out that Ford's "best known act of compassion has been the Nixon pardon."[3] Even so, *Commonweal* published a collection of articles in which the case was made for each candidate. Russell J. Kirk, author of *The Conservative Mind* and many other writings, endorsed

Ford because he felt Ford would conduct a prudent caretaker administration, though he stated that Ronald Reagan "would have been a more colorful and vigorous Republican candidate."[4] Lutheran pastor and author Richard J. Neuhaus favored Carter for his sensitivity combined with vision and enormous energy. He felt Carter's election would "signal the sense of new beginnings essential to the democratic experiment."[5] Reed Whittmore made the case for third-party candidate Eugene McCarthy, whom *Commonweal* praised as "a wise and witty politician" who had not received a satisfactory hearing during the campaign.[6] McCarthy had called the Defense Department "the strongest independent power in world affairs," whose actions were "to a large extent beyond the effective control of Congress." McCarthy wanted to know whom a voter could vote for in the two parties who had any interest in changing that arrangement.[7] *Commonweal* felt "forced by the mathematical pragmatics of his (McCarthy's) situation" to look in another direction for their choice, and thus "tilted" to Carter.

Commonweal was pleased with the Carter-Mondale victory.[8] Carter had survived a so-called Catholic problem. His pronunciation of "Eye-talian" drew much media comment, but it was especially his meeting with a committee of six bishops headed by Archbishop Joseph Bernardin, president of the National Conference of Catholic Bishops, that contributed most to the impression of Carter's problem with some elements in the Catholic community. Bernardin said the bishops were "disappointed" that Carter was unwilling to support an abortion amendment. After a later meeting with Ford, they said they were "encouraged" by Ford's support for a states' rights amendment. The rather widespread impression that the bishops had, in effect, endorsed Ford, however, led them to issue a clarification and an explicit rejection of one-issue voting on abortion. The incident helped bring attention to a significant statement by the administrative board of the U.S. Catholic Conference that had called on Catholics to give close attention to eight issues in evaluating the candidates: abortion, the economy, education, food policy, housing, human rights, mass media, and military expenditures.[9] George McGovern had been the first Democratic candidate to lose the Catholic vote when he received only 48 percent to Nixon's 52 percent. Jimmy Carter's close victory over Ford, however, included a 55 percent share of the Catholic vote.[10]

The 1980 Election

By 1979, *Commonweal* was less than enthusiastic about Jimmy Carter's presidency.

> Three years ago Jimmy Carter . . . traveled the nation and promised us a government as good and compassionate and decent as the American people. There were other promises as well: to reduce military spending by $5 to $7 billion a year; to make America the bread basket rather than the arms merchant of the world; to reform the welfare system and reduce unemployment; to radically revise the tax structure—'A disgrace to the human race'; to save the cities . . . and bring civil rights and economic justice to blacks.

His performance, however, had included much backing off from his agenda of social reform. The editors reflected that they had supported him through these years "with what might be described as off-again-on-again muted enthusiasm."[11] Citing an Associated Press poll that showed that only 26 percent of the public thought Carter was doing a good or excellent job, *Commonweal* wrote a cross section of contributors and asked if he should be reelected. Russell Kirk favored Ronald Reagan whom he felt had a better chance of receiving the nomination this time, but Richard Neuhaus stayed with Carter ("I'm enough of a Democrat not to want to hand the election to Reagan."). Some favored Ted Kennedy, Jerry Brown, Sargent Shriver, or others.[12] Meanwhile, the arrival of the presidential primaries found *Commonweal* deeply troubled by the remarks on nuclear war by Republican hopeful George Bush.

Interviewed in the *Los Angeles Times* by Robert Scheer, Bush criticized Carter for removing the MX missile from his budget. The interview continued:

Scheer: Don't you reach a point with these strategic weapons where you can wipe each other out so many times and no one wants to use them or be willing to use them, that it really doesn't matter whether you are ten percent or two percent lower or higher?

Bush: Yes, if you believe there is no such thing as a winner in nuclear exchange, that argument makes a little sense. I don't believe that.

Scheer: How do you win in a nuclear exchange?

Bush: You have a survivability of command and control, survivability of industrial potential, protection of a percentage of your citizens, and you have a capability that inflicts more damage on the opposition that it can inflict upon you. That's the way you can have a winner, and the Soviet Union's planning is based on the ugly concept of a winner in a nuclear exchange.

Scheer: Do you mean like five percent would survive?

Bush: More than that—if everybody fired everything he had, you'd have more than that survive.

Commonweal was troubled that Bush and other strategists were "toying" not only with survival after nuclear war but with the "winnability" of such a war. There were at least two problems with such a view. First, the argument was "caught up in the mirror logic of all deterrence thinking (e.g. if the Soviets believe in "winnability" and we don't believe in "winnability" they may imagine a psychological advantage leading them to make threats, whereas if we too believe in "winnability" then . . . etc.)." Second, these arguments indulged in what John F. Kennedy presidential aide McGeorge Bundy had called "the 'unreal world' of think-tank calculations and simulated warfare, where nuclear 'exchanges' are carefully calibrated and great cities are 'taken out' with all the abstract neatness of removing a chess piece." Rejecting the dangerous illusion fostered by such talk, *Commonweal* saw more wisdom in a Boston meeting of Physicians for Social Responsibility that emphasized that nuclear war would have no winner and would cause far greater devastation than most Americans realized.[13]

George Bush had to settle for the vice-presidential spot on the Republican ticket as Ronald Reagan easily became the nominee for president. *Commonweal* advised that Carter-Mondale and all Democrats "would be wise to run scared" since they were going into the November race "with the economic issues heavily weighted against them."[14] Aside from this comment, *Commonweal* was rather detached editorially from the 1980 presidential candidates. The magazine published articles of support for each of them. Thomas E. Cronin, a political scientist, explained that Carter was a man of caution, compromise, and compassion who deserved reelection, "not the mindless and condescending contempt so often visited upon him by people with unfair, unrealistic, and misguided standards for judging presidential performance."[15] Theologian Michael Novak wrote that although he was a Democrat—and intended to remain one—he was for Reagan because Reagan had seized the traditional Democratic position of concern for a growing economy. This concern and Reagan's internationalism based on military preparedness had Novak looking forward to the "implacable affability of Ronald Reagan."[16] Richard C. Wade, an urban historian, expressed his support for independent candidate John Anderson. He found Carter reckless in his abortive attempt to rescue the American hostages in Iran and found Reagan "surely not a figure for the eighties."[17]

Most voters did, however, feel that it was "time for a change" and listed this as their reason for supporting Reagan. *Commonweal* said that the election was "not a referendum on conservatism and liberalism." The conservatives' persistent efforts to capture the Republican party had simply given them control of one of the two alternatives—that is, the two major political parties—that the people have. Once the Democrats fell victim to the people's desire for change, there was only one choice. Reagan, the editors stated, would have the advantage of entering office with the confidence of the business community, something Jimmy Carter had spent three years trying to achieve. "That alone may stimulate some badly needed investment and reduce the inflationary behavior that springs from distrust about the economy's long term prospects."[18] The general electorate gave Reagan 51 percent of the vote, Carter 43 percent, and Anderson 6 percent. Reagan drew 48 percent of the Catholic vote compared with 43 percent for Carter and 9 percent for Anderson. After being widely accused of tilting toward Ford on the abortion issue in 1976, the American Catholic bishops held no meetings with the candidates and were intentionally quiet.[19]

Commonweal regarded Reagan's economic plans dubiously. Cutting "big government" down to size and stimulating productivity through a broad tax cut did, however, have popular appeal. It also had psychological possibilities. It was clear and simple, and if enough people thought it would work, it would "set in motion a pattern of expectations and behavior that would be salutary." White House spokesman Edwin Meese described the president's program as "maybe eighty percent psychological." *Commonweal* was mainly concerned that both the tax cuts and the budget cuts be done fairly. The editors felt that it should not be a redistribution of wealth and power to the rich.[20]

Commonweal was more blunt in its criticism of the Reagan administration's essentially military solution for El Salvador. In an editorial entitled "Into El Quagmire," the magazine argued that the Salvadoran insurrection was homegrown not, as the administration maintained, an imported international communist conspiracy. Alexander Haig's proposals for funding and advisors would simply improve "the quality of official terror in El Salvador with the latest U.S. technology." The editorial concluded: "In 1932, when Salvador's military leaders massacred 30,000 peasants, the U.S. government looked the other way. This time they'll be doing it with our weapons and our advisors."[21]

The 1984 Election

"Our work is not finished," said Ronald Reagan in announcing his candidacy for reelection in 1984. *Commonweal* agreed that more had been promised than had been delivered, although the editors acknowledged that an economic recovery was "unquestionably here at last." They found neither party, however, ready to deal responsibly with the spiraling federal budget deficits. Further, they noted the power of Reagan's personality and his "incomparable talent for articulating his plans and deeds in terms of deep-rooted national sentiments."

> Mr. Reagan's America is a giant little house on the prairie, struggling through the locust years, fighting off the Indians, always firm in prayer and song around the family hearth.

While some felt that this simply showed the president's capacity to spread his illusions to others, *Commonweal* said that "at least it is a vision, and it will have to be met with a vision of equal power." Many Americans "suspect that the country and the world don't really work the way that their apple-cheeked and crinkly-eyed leader, by maxim and anecdote, insists. But they haven't yet encountered an alternative that comes as close to matching their instincts."[22]

Later in the campaign *Commonweal* commented on Reagan's preaching of his own version of civil religion. The magazine saw such generalized religious talk as "reintroducing an alienated segment of believing Americans into public life." Further, the editors felt there was a striking amount of intolerance toward religious belief that was particularly frustrating because it was frequently displayed by those who "hold themselves as models of tolerance and open mindedness." They cited specific instances of religious intolerance in the *Nation,* which had rather positively quoted Diderot's remark that "Mankind shall not be free until that last king is strangled with the entrails of the last priest," and in the *New*

York Times, which *Commonweal* said "regularly displays an extraordinary capacity for both obtusity and superiority when dealing with matters which touch upon religion." (It is to the *Times*'s credit that the writer of these words, Peter Steinfels, would subsequently become the senior religion correspondent for the *Times,* but more of that later). *Commonweal,* however, opposed Reagan's call for "voluntary" organized prayer in public schools as "simply double-talk and a real threat to conscience." The editors also critiqued the excesses of Reagan's civil religion that turned into "the ardent elevation of the American Way of Life, of which our particular beliefs are presumed to be only superficial variations." They concluded that they were "ready to love and serve our nation but not worship it. Yes, ours is a jealous God."[23]

The Democratic party provided a number of surprises in the 1984 campaign. Jesse Jackson aroused African-American political consciousness in launching a serious bid for the party's presidential nomination. Geraldine Ferraro became not only the first woman but also the first Italian-American to be nominated for the second-highest office. Walter Mondale boldly announced his intention to raise taxes to meet the mounting deficit. *Commonweal* noted all these developments, including the way the candidacy of Ferraro, as both a Roman Catholic and a pro-choice advocate, had brought the abortion issue renewed media attention. *Commonweal* felt that what *Roe v. Wade* had sanctioned by way of a massive resort to abortion had to be reversed, but there was "more than one position that a Catholic politician can take, in keeping with good church tradition, about the role of government in that reversal." The editors worried, however, that Ferraro's position had roots "in the conventional liberalism that would pigeonhole concern about the value of fetal life as a matter solely of religion and take refuge in the individualistic shibboleth about not imposing beliefs."[24] In the same issue, David R. Carlin, a senator in the Rhode Island state legislature commented that politicians who were both liberal and anti-abortion had "a microscopically small constituency."

> The liberals will disown you, since you can't be one
> of them without being a feminist, and you can't be

a feminist without being pro-choice. And the conservatives won't receive you, since no matter how right you may be on the abortion question, you're still wrong, from their point of view, on a hundred and one other questions . . . The simple fact is that if Geraldine Ferraro had elected to be an anti-abortion liberal there's not a chance in the world she would have attained her elevated status. . . . None of this is to suggest that there is anything insincere or merely expedient about Rep. Ferraro's pro-choice stand. We politicians, like almost everyone else in the world, normally believe sincerely in those positions which it is expedient for us to adopt.[25]

On March 22, 1984, the administrative board of the U.S. Catholic Conference issued "Political Responsibility: Choices for the '80s," which was similar to their 1976 statement. The board said that they did not seek the formation of a religious voting block, nor did it wish to instruct persons on how they should vote by endorsing candidates. It did recommend, however, consideration of the issues of abortion, arms control and disarmament, capital punishment, civil rights, the economy, education, energy, family life, food and agricultural policy, guaranteed health care, housing, human rights, mass media, and regional conflicts in the world, specifically in Central America, the Middle East, and southern Africa.[26]

Controversy erupted, however, when Archbishop John O'Connor of New York seemed to follow a single-issue approach when he said, "I don't see how a Catholic in good conscience can vote for a candidate who explicitly supports abortion."[27] This led to an hour-long meeting between O'Connor and Mario Cuomo, the governor of New York. Cuomo explained that he was personally opposed to abortion but was sworn to uphold the law that allows it. He told O'Connor that he felt that the archbishop had no business telling people how to vote. O'Connor countered that he hadn't been telling people how to vote and that it was "foolish" for anyone to suggest that he had. Later, Cuomo was at home with his wife and young son watching the evening news. In a segment from a televised press conference with

Archbishop O'Connor, a reporter from a Catholic publication asked the archbishop whether he thought Cuomo should be excommunicated. Cuomo recalled his feelings:

> I felt sick. I felt like throwing up. I hoped the Archbishop would say "that's ridiculous." He didn't say that. He said, "Well, we'd have to be very careful, and we'd have to think about it, and we'd have to explore it"—which was by acquiescence, by nonrebuttal a kind of acceptance of the remark. The Archbishop subsequently called me and said he regretted that it didn't come over the way he wanted it to, and had made a statement the next day saying "Of course that's silly, he's a good man and a good Catholic." But it was too late. . . . Personally it was a very heavy hit.[28]

Mario Cuomo had come into national prominence with his dramatically successful keynote speech at the 1984 Democratic National Convention. Cuomo, a longtime reader of and occasional writer for *Commonweal*, gave a speech at Notre Dame on September 13, 1984, entitled "Religious Belief and Public Morality: A Catholic Governor's Perspective." He was grateful, he said, for the dialogue that had clarified that the National Conference of Catholic Bishops would not take positions for or against political candidates and that their stand on specific issues should not be perceived as an expression of political partisanship. He spoke as a Catholic lay person "attached to the church first by birth, then by choice, now by love." He maintained that "while we always owe our bishops' words respectful attention and careful consideration, the question whether to engage the political system in a struggle to have it adopt certain articles of our belief as part of public morality is not a matter of doctrine; it is a matter of prudential political judgment." He said that he accepted church teaching on abortion and believed fetal life should be protected, but "there is no church teaching that mandates the best political course . . . so the Catholic trying to make moral and prudent judgments in the political realm must discern which, if any, of the actions one could take would be best." Cuomo felt that a constitutional amendment was not the best way to deal with the problem of abortion. "Given present attitudes, it would be Prohibition revisited, legislating what couldn't be enforced, and in the process creating a disrespect for law in general." Furthermore, he continued, a constitutional prohibition would likely "allow people to ignore the causes of many abortions instead of addressing them." He felt that the approval or rejection of legal restrictions on abortion should not be the exclusive litmus test of Catholic loyalty. "We should understand that whether abortion is outlawed or not, our work has barely begun: the work of creating a society where the right to life doesn't end at the moment of birth." Cuomo challenged Catholics, whom polls showed to be as accepting of abortion as their non-Catholic neighbors, to resist assimilation "into a larger, blander culture, abandoning the practice of the specific values that made us different." Instead of trying to make laws for others to live by, Catholics, Cuomo maintained, should lead by example, "by living the laws already written for us by God, in our hearts and our minds." He concluded:

> We can be fully Catholic: proudly, totally at ease with ourselves, a people in the world, transforming it, a light to this nation. Appealing to the best in our people not the worst. Persuading not coercing. Leading people to truth by love. And still, all the while, respecting and enjoying our unique pluralistic democracy. And we can do it even as politicians.[29]

In the question period that followed, Cuomo was asked how he could oppose the death penalty and yet not try to change the abortion laws, a question *Commonweal* also raised.[30] Cuomo said he felt that both the death penalty and an anti-abortion amendment would be ineffective because they do not, in practice, alter people's behavior. Furthermore, as governor of New York he already had "voted" on the death penalty when he vetoed the bill reinstating it—which the state legislature had not been able to override—but, he added, "I cannot vote out of existence *Roe v. Wade*."[31]

Reaction to Cuomo's speech was varied. The chairman of the Department of Theology at Notre Dame, Father Richard P.

McBrien, said that "rarely if ever has a public official—Catholic or otherwise—addressed the issue of religious belief and public morality in so sophisticated and nuanced a manner."[32] Author and syndicated columnist Garry Wills agreed, calling it "a thoughtful performance—and a thousand times more nuanced than John Kennedy's single distinction between his faith and his oath back in 1960."[33]

Ralph McInerny, professor of philosophy at Notre Dame and editor of *Catholicism in Crisis,* said Cuomo was wrong "even on his preferred ground of consensus politics."[34] Father Theodore M. Hesburgh, C.S.C., the president of Notre Dame, called Cuomo's talk "brilliant" but added that he thought, and the polls indicated, that there was a possibility of consensus for a somewhat more restrictive but not absolutely prohibitive law.[35] Illinois Republican member of the House of Representatives, Henry J. Hyde, speaking on September 24 at Notre Dame, found Cuomo's position insufficient, and he called on public officials to make clear that abortion is not at bottom a "'Catholic issue' but rather a moral and civil rights issue, a humanitarian issue and a constitutional issue of the first importance."[36] *Commonweal* commended Cuomo for courageously risking "what few politicians will in this age of TV clips—complexity," but asked, at the same time, if consensus was as impossible as it seemed to Mr. Cuomo? Was there not more that "a prominent Democrat like Cuomo could do to move his party away from its one-sided stance on this issue?" Cuomo had, however, clearly "moved a public debate beyond slogans, fingerpointing and electioneering."[37] *Commonweal* columnist Abigail McCarthy said that whether one agreed with Governor Cuomo or not, what he had done was to articulate a position based on a longstanding *Commonweal* tradition of respect for the lay person's work in the world, that is, his or her "lay vocation." If being a "Commonweal Catholic" meant anything, suggested McCarthy, it meant that one saw "the lay person's work as his or her responsibility—as that for which he or she has competence by reason of training and experience." Vatican II's *Decree on the Laity* had endorsed this viewpoint. Cuomo's views were those of a mature and religiously integrated Catholic politician. McCarthy felt that the "shabby" way the "discussion" with Archbishop O'Connor had developed in the public press indicated a church in which there was "a tragic disregard for the bonds that should unite its members in reverence and love," one in which there was "no machinery for consulting with a lay person in a particular area of competence, and, in any case, little or no will to do so."[38]

The abortion discussion played out several more scenes in the drama of the 1984 campaign.[39] Archbishop O'Connor attacked Geraldine Ferraro for a 1982 statement she had made about the Catholic position on abortion being "not mono-lithic." O'Connor charged that this was a misrepresentation of Catholic teaching. Ferraro argued that she was not talking about the church's position, but about the position of American Catholics. This led Catholics for a Free Choice to take a full-page ad in the *New York Times* on October 7, 1984, with the sixty-point headline: A DIVERSITY OF OPINIONS REGARDING ABORTION EXISTS AMONG COMMITTED CATHOLICS. Later, the Sacred Congregation for Religious and Secular Institutes (SCRIS) took action against two dozen women and one man in religious orders who had signed the ad. SCRIS said they must publicly retract their adherence to the statement or suffer expulsion from their orders. *Commonweal* editor Peter Steinfels tried to interpret how SCRIS had managed to box itself and the church into such a no-win situation and speculated that they "simply didn't understand the American situation" and had "never thought through the consequences of its action."

Consider this. With one master stroke SCRIS has (a) resurrected a forgotten statement from the dustheap of abortion manifestoes; (b) shifted attention from the issue of abortion to the issue of free speech and intellectual integrity (which is more or less what the ad wanted to do in the first place); (c) put Catholics for a Free Choice center stage and made them beneficiary of sympathy for the penalized signers; (d) provided substance to the ad's claim that behind the appearance of Catholic opposition to abortion lurks the fear of ecclesiastical sanctions, whether of hellfire or expulsion from one's religious order; (e) made it more difficult for

Catholic liberals and feminists to part company with their liberal and feminist associates on the question of abortion.

So harmful to the church and to the anti-abortion cause was the SCRIS action that Steinfels entitled his editorial "Is Rome Anti-Catholic?"[40] A number of statements by individual bishops and groups of bishops were issued as election day approached. Bishop James Malone of Youngstown, Ohio, the president of the National Conference of Catholic Bishops, issued statements on August 9 and on October 14 that were substantive and even-handed.[41] Archbishop Bernard Law of Boston was joined by seventeen New England bishops in a statement on September 4 that called abortion "the critical issue of the moment" and commented that "while nuclear holocaust is a future possibility, the holocaust of abortion is a present reality."[42] On October 22, Auxiliary Bishop Thomas Gumbleton of Detroit and twenty-three other bishops countered that "to claim that nuclear war was only a potential evil and that abortion is actual neglects a terrible reality. For indeed, there can be no possibility of exercising moral responsibility against nuclear war if we wait until the missiles have been released."[43] Archbishop O'Connor spoke again on October 15 and linked his concern for abortion to other life issues and emphasized that no one should be mistaken about the bishops' unanimity on the abortion question.[44] Joseph Cardinal Bernardin, speaking at Georgetown University on October 25, defended the "consistent ethic of life" or the "seamless garment approach that linked together abortion, peace, poverty, civil rights and opposition to U.S. policies in Central America."[45]

Ronald Reagan won easily over Walter Mondale in the 1984 election, with an eighteen-point edge in the national electorate. Reagan received 56 percent of the Catholic vote, an all-time high for a Republican nominee. Analysis seemed to indicate that the protracted public quarrel over abortion that involved various Catholic prelates, Geraldine Ferraro, and others was not a major factor in the election. The CBS–*New York Times* poll found that only 8 percent of Catholics said that abortion was one of the top issues affecting their vote. Among those 8 percent, 71 percent voted for Reagan and 28 percent for Mondale. The major issues that concerned all voters were arms control and defense and the economy.[46] *Commonweal* presented no immediate editorial comment on the outcome of the election. Occasional columnist Nancy Amidei, former director of the Food Research and Action Center in Washington, D.C., pointed out that election results in the Senate and House of Representatives showed good news for those concerned with "fairness" issues.[47] Also, a *Commonweal* letter writer, commenting on Geraldine Ferraro's experiences during the campaign, stated:

> Does anyone imagine that Catholic "truth squads" would systematically disrupt the rallies of a candidate who was either male or a Protestant? An almost certain outcome of these assaults is that the next female candidate for national office will not be a Catholic. No party would voluntarily saddle itself with such a handicap. How ironic that what Mondale hath loosed in San Francisco, Archbishop O'Connor hath rebound in New York.[48]

Meanwhile, *Commonweal* columnist John Garvey wondered about the same liberals who applauded the Catholic bishops for their stand on nuclear weapons but were appalled when Archbishop O'Connor said that he didn't see how a Catholic in good conscience could vote for someone who openly advocated abortion. Garvey doubted that the same outrage would be provoked if O'Connor had said, "I don't see how a Catholic can in good conscience vote for someone who is prepared to destroy civilian population during wartime."[49]

Political scientist Mary C. Segers saw the 1984 election somewhat differently, pointing out that it had revealed "what might be called the underside of American Catholicism." She referred to "the openly partisan attacks on Ferraro" by some bishops:

> The American electorate was treated to the streetcorner spectacle of the archbishop of New York, in full episcopal regalia, attacking in partisan fashion the Democratic vice-presidential candidate while

neglecting to say anything about the positions of the Republican candidates. And O'Connor was not alone. After organizers invited Ferraro to march in Philadelphia's Columbus Day parade, John Cardinal Krol threatened to pull out all the Catholic schools and bands if Ferraro marched. So she withdrew, thus allowing Philadelphia organizers to avoid a confrontation with Krol.

Segers also mentioned the statement of the New England bishops, led by Archbishop Bernard Law, that singled out abortion as the central issue in the campaign in such a way that it was "tantamount to an endorsement of the Republican ticket." Ferraro has recorded her surprise and incredulity in the face of these events in her memoir of the campaign, *Ferraro: My Story* (Bantam, 1985). Segers finds Ferraro's incredulity justified for four reasons. First, Ferraro was criticized for holding the same position on abortion policy that the most prominent male Catholic politicians in America— such as Senators Kennedy and Moynihan and House Speaker "Tip" O'Neill—had held without challenge by the hierarchy for over a decade. Second, neither John F. Kennedy nor any previous Catholic candidate for high national office had been treated the way Ferraro was. Third, the National Conference of Catholic Bishops had specifically cautioned against such a single-issue approach in the election. Fourth, although the bishops had issued a highly publicized pastoral letter on war and peace in 1983, they said "precious little" about arms control, defense expenditures, and the nuclear freeze during the 1984 campaign and deliberately postponed the release of the first draft of their economics pastoral letter until a week after the election so as to appear nonpartisan. "No such restraint characterized the actions of certain bishops on the abortion question," said Segers. Placing the Ferraro candidacy in the context of the continued exclusion of women from American politics, Segers pointed out, helped her to appreciate the "seriousness of the bishops' error."

While women are a majority (53 percent) of the population, they hold only 14 percent of the state legislative seats, 4 percent of the gubernatorial posts, and only 5 percent of the congressional seats. . . . In this context, the Democratic party's nomination of Ferraro as the first female vice-presidential candidate represented a significant advance in the struggle for political equality. Were the American Catholic hierarchy fully committed to the struggle for equality and equity for women, I suspect they would have refrained from the excesses of a partisan, single issue attack on Ferraro.[50]

The 1988 Election

During the 1988 presidential campaign, *Commonweal* was rather quiet in terms of editorial comment. The magazine did hire, however, Fred Siegel, author of *Troubled Journey: From Pearl Harbor to Ronald Reagan* (Hill and Wang, 1984), to write a series of articles on the election.[51]

The editors also pointed out the historic change manifest at the Democratic National Convention in Atlanta.[52] In 1964, when Jesse Jackson was only twenty-two years old, duly elected black delegates were denied entrance to the Democrats' convention hall in Atlantic City. Now, only two-and-a-half decades later, Jackson himself was "a pivotal figure for the Democrats, acclaimed, feared, wooed; not merely a delegate but a credible national candidate. Social change rarely moves at such a pace." They praised Jackson's speech that had "appealed to what is best in Americans: common sense and common ground, interdependence, compassion for the poor and weak, religious faith and hope, belief in hard work and opportunity for all." Jackson's refrain "we can do better than that" was applied to the self-destructiveness of drugs and to a cynicism, fear, and violence that was beneath our dignity. His refrain to the downtrodden—"I understand"—carried, said *Commonweal*, "a credibility that few public figures can match." Knowing the delegate count, he "was free to mention marginalized groups like gays and lesbians and to speak to the needs of ignored minorities like the handicapped and the uninsured." Jackson had spoken simple truths, asserting that most poor people work hard every day and still can't make ends meet and that a war on drugs can't be fought until we are willing to challenge the bankers and the gun sellers. Overall, the editors found the speech "a moment to be celebrated, remembered, enlarged."[53]

Fred Siegel presented an analysis of the foundering campaign of Michael Dukakis as the election approached.[54] Both in style and content, the Massachusetts governor conveyed an increasingly marginalized "legalitarian liberalism." Franklin Delano Roosevelt could proudly proclaim that the "one great difference that has characterized the division (between liberals and conservatives) has been that the liberal party—no matter what its particular name was at the time—believes in the efficacy of the will of the great majority of the people as distinguished from the judgment of a small minority." The political problem for the Democrats, said Siegel, was that this was no longer true.

When the results were in at the polls, *Commonweal* pointed out that Dukakis had done better than Jimmy Carter in 1980 or Walter Mondale in 1984, including among Catholic voters. But better wasn't best. And so, Bush it was, "with the nation's prayers for his continuing good health," an obvious reference to the winner's running mate, J. Danforth Quayle.[55] *Commonweal* columnist David R. Carlin stated that the Bush campaign was shamefully demagogic, but its demagoguery was adroit. "In attacking Dukakis, the Bush camp found just the right symbols to arouse the latent fear and loathing millions of Americans have for the newer school of liberalism."[56] Siegel said that Jesse Jackson had hurt the Democrats and his own claims to be not just a protest candidate by refusing to bow out of the primaries when it was clear that he had lost in eight consecutive states. "By continuing to campaign after he was decisively defeated, Jackson created an undertow that dragged Dukakis away from his impending clash with George Bush." Siegel's analysis, however, attributed most of the blame to Dukakis himself and to the Democratic party. He gave former Minnesota senator Hubert H. Humphrey the last word on Dukakis's and the Democrats' failure to build a post–New Deal presidential politics.

In 1975 Humphrey was told that his brand of liberalism had been criticized as passé by the newly elected governor of Massachusetts, Michael Dukakis. The last Democratic nominee who could be called a regular guy replied: "You know there are two kinds of liberals. Dukakis is a process liberal, and I'm not. All he cares is that the pipeline is neat and shiny and clean. He doesn't care if shit comes out the other end. But me, I don't care if the pipeline is cracked and rusty and shitty so long as the right results come out the other end. That's the difference between us."

How right you were, Hubert![57]

The *Commonweal* editors, somewhat more elegantly, warned that it was "as political and economic liberals that Democrats once made their mark and their contribution" and that they "ought to prepare themselves to do so again, after four years of George Bush."[58]

3

Commonweal Itself

While the parade of presidential politics marched forward through the 1970s and 1980s, what was going on with *Commonweal* itself and its editors?

The most important change in *Commonweal* came just after its fiftieth anniversary in 1974 when it shifted from weekly to biweekly publication. Subscriptions and advertising were holding up well, but inflation made it necessary, the editors maintained, to "cut costs substantially, and the only way we have been able to devise is to join the ranks of such magazines as the *National Review, Christianity and Crisis,* the *New Leader,* the *Saturday Review/World,* and other well known biweeklies."[1] The economics of less frequent publication made possible the addition of extra pages to make a fatter issue, and the overall result was a reduction of only 20 percent in the annual total number of pages. The new biweekly *Commonweal* contained thirty-two pages per issue.

The major staff change took place in September 1978 when John Deedy left and Peter Steinfels arrived as executive editor. Deedy had been managing editor since May 1967. He moved to Massachusetts's North Shore to give himself completely to independent writing. "News and Views," his chatty and sometimes contentious column of tidbits that had long been a feature in *Commonweal*, departed with him. In his parting comment, Deedy told readers to "look forward to change here (in *Commonweal*)." He said that turnover in an organization as small as *Commonweal* inevitably translated to real change, however subtle. "The time ahead should be an interesting one for *Commonweal* readers. I am anticipating it as much as I hope you will."[2] Publisher Edward S. Skillin has described Deedy as "the liberal voice with a capital L" and pointed out that he was "more liberal than Peter (Steinfels) or Jim (O'Gara)."[3] *Commonweal* gave parting thanks to Deedy for his years with the magazine, years that saw the fragmentation of American liberalism and the evaporation of post-Conciliar optimism, noting that "through it all, John Deedy carried on in a style that matched militancy with good humor, a zest for combat with personal gentleness, and a refusal to take it all too seriously."[4]

Peter Steinfels had been an editor at *Commonweal* from 1964 to 1972, having joined the magazine after his graduation from Loyola University, Chicago. Since 1972, he had completed a doctorate in European history, directed a program dealing with humanities, ethics, and the life sciences, and edited the *Hastings Center Report*. He had written articles and reviews for numerous journals, edited a book of essays on death and dying, and contributed a regular column to *Commonweal*. *The Neo-Conservatives: The Men Who Are Changing America's Politics*, his incisive and critical book on neo-conservatism, would appear in 1979. As executive editor he would, in addition to regular editorial functions, have special responsibilities for long-range editorial and financial planning.[5]

Steinfels brought with him to his new position long years of association with *Commonweal*. He had in fact grown up in a Chicago household where *Commonweal* was part of the regular reading fare of the family and was well aware of *Commonweal* during his undergraduate years at Loyola University. He joined the magazine in 1964 when he came to New York and began studying at Columbia University for his Ph.D. in history. The *Commonweal* editorial staff has always been remarkably small and included at that time only Edward Skillin, James O'Gara, Daniel Callahan, and John Leo.

Steinfels had witnessed a number of editorial debates at the magazine over the years. He had been present, for rexample, in 1967 and 1968 when the Jim O'Gara–Dan Callahan key confrontation erupted over Catholic identity and the future direction *Commonweal* should take.[6] In 1972, he joined Callahan at the Institute for Society, Ethics and the Life Sciences but continued to write a regular column for the magazine through the 1970s. On the O'Gara-Callahan clash, Steinfels has stated that he felt that the success of *Commonweal* should be measured in terms of the *Nation,* the *New Republic,* and the *New York Review of Books,* and not in terms of *America,* the *National Catholic Reporter,* and *U.S. Catholic* but that "at least in my mind that didn't necessarily mean that Catholic identity was minimized as it might have meant in Dan's (Callahan's) mind." Viewing that late 1960s episode retrospectively, Steinfels reflected that "just as you can look back and say that on Catholic identity Jim's (O'Gara's) view may have been sounder than Dan's (Callahan's), you can see that Ed's (Skillin's) more cautious financial approach may have been sounder than whatever Dan dreamed of."[7]

Steinfels's early roots with *Commonweal* were evident in "Death of a Hero," a column he wrote in 1976 on the occasion of the death of John Cogley. "As an adolescent," wrote Steinfels, "I admired many people; but Cogley, known to me only through his columns in *Commonweal*, I wanted to be like. Sometime during high school I wrote a letter listing my lifetime ambitions. To write a column like Cogley's in *Commonweal* was one of them."[8]

Cogley worked as an editor at *Commonweal* from 1949 to 1955, served as a columnist until 1964, and then contributed regularly after that. His death at age sixty was commemorated with a sampler of his decades of writing in the magazine.[9] Many readers, and obviously the young Peter Steinfels, had identified strongly with the elegant simplicity and humility of

style with which Cogley took positions of courage and integrity through those years. Though Cogley separated from the magazine and in some ways separated from Roman Catholicism with his entry into the Episcopal church in 1973 (he had become a deacon and was awaiting ordination to the priesthood at the time of his death), his death was a major marker in the history of *Commonweal*. Ten years later, in 1986, James O'Gara wrote an appreciative remembrance of Cogley, his friend and colleague since their youthful collaboration in running a Catholic Worker House of Hospitality in Chicago before World War II. In the piece entitled "In the Thick of It: Honesty, Intellect and Friendship," O'Gara recalled Cogley as a colleague, friend, devoted husband, and father. He "was a good man, a very good man."[10]

In 1977, another giant in *Commonweal*'s history, George N. Shuster, died at eighty-two. Shuster's first writing in *Commonweal* (then known as *The Commonweal*) appeared on December 3, 1924, in the fourth issue of the magazine. He soon became an editor and acted as the managing editor under founding editor Michael Williams, from 1926 to 1937. Shuster broke with Williams over the latter's (and the American Catholic press in general's) uncritical support of Franco in the Spanish Civil War. The incident eventually resulted in *Commonweal* changing editors and direction in March 1938. Edward Skillin, *Commonweal*'s publisher, who had been hired by Shuster in 1933 and who, along with Philip Burnham, became its coeditor in 1938, wrote an essay on Shuster's life. He recalled Shuster's early critique of Hitler and the Nazis, his enrichment of the American Catholic cultural scene by introducing to American readers in *Commonweal* leading representatives of European Catholic thought, his more than twenty books, and his long career in public service and in higher education. Skillin wrote that he thought Shuster would probably be remembered "more for the stances that he took than for his remarkable productiveness and versatility."

Skillin quoted Father Theodore Hesburgh's funeral homily on George Shuster, as "a great and gentle man."[11]

Creative Affirmation of Tradition

Shuster and Cogley were important parts of a long and honorable *Commonweal* tradition of distinction. Editor Jim O'Gara and publisher Ed Skillin had that tradition and a concern for its future very much in mind when hiring Peter Steinfels as executive editor in 1978 and, in adding to his regular editorial functions, a special responsibility for long-range editorial and financial planning. Peter Steinfels had the strongest individual influence at *Commonweal* during the period from 1978 to 1988.

Upon his return, Steinfels immediately drafted a memo that was, in one sense, a statement of what he was coming back to *Commonweal* to try to do. The memo went through various drafts as it was shared, initially with a group of Catholic intellectuals and activists, and finally, in letter form, with all subscribers. An early version began with this statement: "At no other time has there been such a special need—and a special opportunity—for a Catholic intellectual journal like *Commonweal*." Steinfels asserted that Catholic intellectual life was in profound disarray, at a time when one might have expected it to be enjoying a new vigor. The letter delivered both good news and bad news. The good news was that the educational and scholarly goals regarding the quality of American Catholic intellectual life that were yearned for and debated in the decades before Vatican II were now accomplished facts. Catholics were well beyond the national mean for college attendance and were proportionately represented on the faculties at even the most elite universities. Younger Catholic faculty members were as likely to hold tenure, publish frequently, and identify themselves as "intellectuals" as their peers from Protestant backgrounds. Irish Catholics had the highest educational achievement of any group except Jews. Even in forums often considered "quintessentially secular," individual Catholic intellectuals were highly visible. In effect, the constituency once known as *Commonweal* Catholics had grown markedly. The bad news, however, was that this potential constituency, this growing intellectual and cultural presence seemed "less and less likely to carry with it a distinctly Catholic identity, to contribute to the Church's own tasks of self-definition and proclamation, to maintain a Catholic-Christian tradition only now being renewed by its long delayed encounter with modernity."[12]

Steinfels saw an equal disarray in the intellectual and cultural life generally. There was, he felt, a wide recognition that the malaise demanded analyses and remedies that were not narrowly political or economic, but moral and even religious. Yet a Catholic contribution was barely forthcoming.

> The moment would seem to be propitious for those commenting out of a tradition like the Catholic one, with its balance between immanence and transcendence, between individual and community, between intellectual analysis and ritual, between responsibility to the social order, contemplation, and eschatalogical hope. Is this also the moment, ironically, when the discontinuities between generations of educated Catholics may possibly reach the point where much of that tradition becomes irrecoverable?[13]

The role of *Commonweal* in such a context was obvious. Catholic intellectuals and those holding a special adherence to Catholic experience and thought needed the forum and stimulus that a first-rate Catholic journal of opinion could provide. Catholic intellectuals were dispersed and in many cases demoralized and yet, wrote Steinfels, "perhaps more than ever capable of significant contribution to American intellectual and cultural life." *Commonweal* had the tradition and strength for such a task, but had weaknesses too. It was a shoestring operation. Money was tight. Thus, the magazine could not operate as the receptive forum of a somewhat naturally formed community. To a large extent it had to actively create that community. Larger writers' fees, improvements in format, and aggressive promotion might boost circulation, which would, in turn, help finances. No radical improvement, however, could occur "without a breakthrough in finances." In addition to money, two other things were needed: hard and imaginative editing and contacts of every sort. The burden, to be sure, would fall mostly on the present editors, but assistance from friends could help with concrete and realistic proposals of ideas as well as tips on works-in-progress. Friends could also help with contacts to produce contributors of money, names of potential writers, and suggestions for occasions where knowledge of *Commonweal* might be advanced.

If *Commonweal* could mobilize money, editorial talent, and a network of supporters, it could, offered Steinfels, "reknot ties, kindle loyalty, focus attention." It could, in short, "render significant service to those who, in a wide variety of ways, feel themselves attached to Catholicism, to the Church itself, to the society in general." If, however, *Commonweal* could not mobilize these forces, the loss might affect "at least a generation of the kind of leadership the journal has previously nourished; the loss may, in fact, be permanent."[14]

Steinfels's draft generated some interesting feedback. Father Philip Murnion, a New York-based national leader of parish renewal efforts, said he "found the dour tone of the early pages unhappy." There were serious problems, but he saw them as reverse sides of good new developments. "The independent achievement of the Catholic intellectual and his/her full acceptance into the community of intellectual life in the U.S. probably required a certain distance from the church, however unfortunate that may be." He felt, however, that there ought to be many points where a new relationship could be forged. He also reminded Steinfels "to include in your concerns Catholics who are not intellectuals but who are significant in the making of our society." Ed Marciniak, a veteran Catholic lay leader in Chicago, expressed concern about a "strident" tone in *Commonweal* that he felt might alienate what he considered a potential audience. He tried to differentiate between stridency and taking a strong position, even if that meant issuing a healthy polemic every now and then. Michael True, who had written frequently for the magazine, felt *Commonweal* should give closer attention to the arts, which were mentioned only generally in the Steinfels memo. Sociologist William McCready said that a basic problem for *Commonweal* was that the Catholic church had managed to alienate much of its natural support in the Catholic intellectual subculture "simply by ignoring them and their concerns." Dan Callahan favored an immediate major change in editorial personnel, starting with Peter Steinfels becoming the editor. It is difficult to see how this could have been achieved, however, even if Steinfels were disposed to do this. He was an employee, not the owner of *Commonweal.* Jim O'Gara and Ed Skillin discussed the possibility of Steinfels's becoming editor in the future, but even that was not absolutely guaranteed. Callahan told Steinfels that it was unrealistic to expect that people not at the magazine on a daily basis would be very helpful with ideas or leads. He felt too that the practical pitch in the memo was "both weak and vague." David J. O'Brien, a leading Catholic intellectual and historian, commended the basic analysis in the Steinfels memo and added that he shared it "wholeheartedly." He suggested a tour of major cities with the document, making an appeal to a small number of well-to-do Catholics. This would have been similar to the successful tour made by founding editor Michael Williams before *Commonweal* was launched in 1924.[15]

In the end, no such tour was undertaken, perhaps because, as William McCready had suggested, "much of the economic resources which would be available to a journal like *Commonweal* are held by conservatives who would not be terribly interested in the product."[16] The major advantage of the memo may have been the fresh articulation of purpose and identity that it gave to *Commonweal,* especially for Peter Steinfels himself, but for others too.

Commonweal received a new look in type and format shortly after Steinfels's return in 1978. An editorial, "New Look for a New Era," explained that, in one sense, the change was only skin deep. *Commonweal* represented for its editors and readers "a loyalty to both the past and future of their church and their society, and a conviction that the best of the past could be nurtured into a better future only by the exercise of a critical, inquiring spirit." This long tradition would continue in the magazine. It would try to deal with what it called two marks of the new era—a change in Catholic religious identity and a change in liberal political identity. Concerning the first the editors commented:

Where educated Catholics had once experienced a sense of common identity arising from their minority status in the church and the suspicion with which they were often held in academic or liberal milieus, the collapse of old barriers now removed further points of self-definition. Assimilation, combined with the frequent failures of church institutions to live up to the high standards of Vatican II, often led, paradoxically, to a new isolation, a loss of contact with Catholic tradition—or, on the other hand, to a muscular effort to maintain ties by reasserting ethnicity or stressing those cultural or political elements that presumably make a special Catholic contribution to American life. Whatever one's judgment on this situation, it is one that will not disappear tomorrow. What was once black or white about being a Catholic will remain gray for an indefinite period to come. A journal like *Commonweal* will have to respond to this fact. It will have to find a place in its pages for exploring the dilemmas of the theologian, the church reformer, the social activist, the searching layperson, the "cultural Catholic."

Concerning the change in liberal political identity, the editorial stated that the struggle for racial equality and the war in Vietnam had raised challenges to the "optimistic, middle-of-the-road, pragmatic liberalism that had dominated Washington since the New Deal." By now, "not only conservatives and radicals, but liberals, too, have mounted effective critiques of many of the interventionist programs, domestic and foreign, that had their roots in the New Deal." *Commonweal* felt, however, that so far little of positive value had emerged from this flux and that there was a grave danger that "an often justified criticism of liberal programs will do nothing more than provide a rationale for dismantling the welfare state, not to the benefit of the poor and vulnerable, but to the gain of other concentrations of power like the giant corporations." If there was no going back to the days of Franklin Delano Roosevelt, there ought also to be no going back to the days of Calvin Coolidge and Herbert Hoover. It was into "this foggy and choppy sea of political identity, as well as of religious identity" that *Commonweal* now set sail.[17]

Some changes occurred in the crew as *Commonweal* moved forward to and into the 1980s. In July 1979, associate editor Raymond A. Schroth, a Jesuit who was the first priest to serve as a *Commonweal* editor, left the magazine to become academic dean of Rockhurst College, the Jesuit liberal arts college in Kansas City, Missouri. Schroth had spent seven-and-a-half years in his part-time position at *Commonweal* while teaching at Fordham University. His primary responsibility was as book review editor, but he also took turns writing editorials.[18] In September 1979, Daniel M. Murtaugh and David Toolan, S.J., joined the *Commonweal* staff as assistant editors.[19] A year later Murtaugh left for a position in the business world but kept his informal ties to *Commonweal* and would play a role in its later evolution.[20] Toolan continued with *Commonweal* until 1989, capably performing the same function as book review editor that Ray Schroth had before him. After sixteen years of service, poetry editor John Fandel left *Commonweal* in December 1979 and was replaced by Rosemary Deen and Marie Ponsot, both of whom taught at Queens College in New York City. Ponsot left in 1985, but Deen stayed.[21]

In March 1984, James O'Gara retired from his position as editor. He had served as managing editor from January 1952 to May 1967 and as editor from that date until March 1984. During these years, he wrote between 750,000 and 1,000,000 words in editorials, in articles, and in the weekly column he did for a few years. In his farewell essay, he recalled that he was a youngish married man with two children when he moved from Chicago to New York to become the managing editor. He was very proud to be asked to join *Commonweal's* staff, for it "stood for something in the American church that I was proud to identify with. It seems easy for some to forget," he recalled, "how much desert there was in the pre–Vatican II church, but I cannot help but remember. And in that desert *Commonweal* was often a lonely voice crying out on behalf of human rights, of ecumenism, of interracial harmony, of social justice, of intellectual integrity." O'Gara's reflection on the phrase *Commonweal* Catholic was especially interesting:

From the time I was old enough to begin to develop some opinions of my own, I have always been what used to be called a "*Commonweal* Catholic*,*" as I am sure many of our readers are too. The term was originally coined by our critics as a denigrating description, to indicate someone whose theology was shaky at best and whose loyalty was dubious, but I never took the term that way. To me the expression meant one who had a definite commitment to the church but who was not sectarian in spirit. The commitment of the "*Commonweal* Catholic" was—and is—to a church that was open and pluralistic, not rigid and authoritarian, a church that was a visible manifestation of Jesus's presence in the world. Thus I saw the description intended to be derogatory as a badge of honor, something to be lived up to, and I still feel the same way today.[22]

Publisher Ed Skillin, regularly working despite being fourteen years older than the sixty-six-year old Jim O'Gara, did not want O'Gara to retire. Although under no pressure from Steinfels to move on, O'Gara felt it was time to have a new generation running the magazine. He also felt very comfortable with Steinfels as his successor. He has described Steinfels as an "ideal Catholic *Commonweal* editor," who had well demonstrated his commitment to the Catholic character of the magazine.[23] Consequently, O'Gara, who has the distinction of being the person who contributed the most words to the magazine's pages, retired as editor in 1984. That he also symbolized *Commonweal* as fair-minded, courageous, and dedicated was made evident in the many letters sent to him on the occasion of his retirement. He received honorary degrees from Loyola University in Chicago and from St. John's University, Collegeville, Minnesota, and praise from the Jesuit weekly *America* and others in the Catholic press. Only the ultraconservative *Wanderer* managed a negative note, stating: "Only small solace (since he will be replaced by another anti-Catholic clone) can be taken from the news that James O'Gara has retired."[24] Among the projects that have occupied O'Gara since his retirement has been a year's stay as a visiting professor at the University of Notre Dame.

In July 1984, Anne Robertson, a veteran of twenty-four years with the magazine, assumed the post of production editor. Patrick Jordan, a former managing editor at the *Catholic Worker,* became an assistant editor, as did Karen Sue Smith, who holds master's degrees from both Notre Dame and the Harvard Divinity School. On the financial front, no great fundraising tours nor major contributors appeared either in the 1979 fund drive or in the 1984 appeal, but steady growth of *Commonweal* Associates, contributors of fifty to two hundred dollars, was achieved, and many smaller contributors came forward. The editors reported that "keeping *Commonweal* alive and vigorous seems to be a matter of banding together many Davids in a world of Goliaths."[25]

4

Some Issues in the Seventies and Eighties

In this section, we will share some plainspoken thoughts on marriage versus living together, catch up with continuing scholarship about the life and faith of the distinguished writer Flannery O'Connor, share novelist Mary Gordon's search for meaningful Marian piety, and hear one of the best known theologians in the United States, Father Richard McBrien, analyze homosexuality and the priesthood. We will then consider an important aspect of *Commonweal*—its columnists—giving particular attention to two of them, John Garvey and Abigail McCarthy, both of whom have been a major presence throughout the 1970s and 1980s.

Marriage versus "Just Living Together"

In a typical year about six hundred unsolicited manuscripts are submitted to *Commonweal* for possible publication. All are carefully evaluated by the editors. In fact, a daily packet of mail is circulated to the editors, keeping them in regular touch with all correspondence. Most manuscripts are declined since

the competition for the scarce space in *Commonweal*'s
twenty-six issues each year is quite intense.

In 1981, Jo McGowan, a young woman from Hoboken,
New Jersey, submitted a manuscript of particular timeliness to
the 1970s and 1980s. It was accompanied by a neatly hand-
written note:

> I enclose an article which may be of interest to you
> . . . it is an article in defense of marriage. In the
> circles in which I travel (the peace movement,
> mainly) marriage is viewed cynically at best. This
> is troubling to me not only because I am Catholic
> and believe in marriage as a sacrament, not only
> because I am married myself and know what a
> wondrous thing it is, but also because I see mar-
> riage as an act with tremendous community-build-
> ing potential . . . or to put it in Christian terms, as a
> step in the direction of the Kingdom.
>
> To build community is something most, if not all,
> of my peace movement friends are deeply commit-
> ted to, and yet most of them have chosen living
> together as the form for the central relationship in
> their lives. Because living together seems to me to
> be a private, individualistic decision—the anti-thesis
> of community—I started to write this article to clar-
> ify, both to them and to myself, what real marriage
> could be. Since then it has broadened in scope and
> now addresses issues that I believe are—or should
> be—central to the lives of all Christians.
>
> I look forward to hearing from you![1]

Commonweal published Jo McGowan's "Marriage Versus
Just Living Together: Acknowledging Life in the Context of
Community" in March 1981. In the article McGowan maintained that apart from anything else, marriage is a very practical institution. "It is an institution that makes allowances for
human failings." Simply living together "does not provide the
security of knowing that this is forever." Her central point was
that marriage was a community-building act, while living
together was not. She described the heavy emphasis placed

on individualism in American culture and commented that it was not surprising that this individualism should be reflected in young people choosing to live together, an essentially private choice. What was surprising was "the extent to which most *marriages* are also quite private affairs, all the while purporting to be community events." After a critique of overblown marriage ceremonies and receptions, she described her own simplified and inclusive wedding and reception and reflected:

> It seemed to us then, and it seems even more so now, that our wedding was a symbol of the way we want to live our lives: surrounded by family and friends; giving and receiving the gifts of time, laughter, advice and help; sharing food, work, prayer, and celebration; creating a world where children are free and full of joy.
>
> But marriage is a community event. It expresses in its ideal form, a belief in the goodness of community, a belief in the beauty of two people who love each other coming together to live in communion, a belief in the wonder of human life, a belief so strong that it expresses itself in the creation of a new human life.[2]

McGowan's article proved to be one of the freshest and most profound treatments of a subject that was curiously neglected in most circles at that time. *Commonweal* quoted the above two paragraphs in promotions to new subscribers to the magazine.[3]

Flannery O'Connor

The growth of information about the late Flannery O'Connor brought pleasure to many *Commonweal* readers during the 1970s and 1980s. In particular, the publication in 1979 of the *Letters of Flannery O'Connor,* a 617-page volume of her correspondence, made available a wealth of new information about the author. The letters made the life and work of this major literary figure of the twentieth century all the more interesting and fascinating. O'Connor was a victim of lupus, bone disintegration, shingles, and anemia. She later developed a tumor, cystitis, and a kidney infection. She died at age thirty-nine, but throughout it all she continued in her dedication to her writing and to her Catholic faith, which was so integral to her being. Robert Phillips wrote in *Commonweal* of her "wicked sense of humor and heavenly capacity for turning a phrase."[4] Her correspondence indicated that she was a constant reader of *Commonweal*. To her spiritually wandering friends she wrote that if they wanted their faith, they had to work for it: "What people don't realize is how much religion costs. They think faith is a big electric blanket, when of course it is the cross."[5] When a relative paid for her to visit Lourdes, she wrote a close correspondent, "About the Lourdes business. I am going as a pilgrim, not a patient. I will not be taking any bath. I am one of those people who could die for his religion easier than take a bath for it."[6]

Searching for the Meaningful Mary

Mary Gordon was a literary figure whose first novel *Final Payments* (1978), published when she was twenty-nine, brought her both critical acclaim and popular success. *Harper's* reviewer Frances Taliaferro called it "a beauty" and "the least pompous novel imaginable on the largest possible subject: Christian charity." Taliaferro found it "a Catholic novel in the same way that *A Portrait of the Artist as a Young Man* by James Joyce is a Catholic novel, which is to say both completely and not at all." *The Company of Women* (1980) further established Gordon's reputation. Her personal religious path was a familiar one. Raised in a devoutly Catholic household, she had rebelled as a teenager and then had a religious coming home as an adult.[7]

Her *Commonweal* essay "Coming to Terms with Mary" was one that spoke to many readers. In it she explained that as a teenager in Queens in the 1960s she was exhorted at prom time to obtain a Mary-like gown. "The Mary-like gown was an invention of the nuns and a coalition of sodalists, and its intent, I think, was to make prom dresses as much like habits as possible." She experienced Mary as "a stick to beat smart girls with."

Her example was held up constantly: an example of silence, of subordination, of the pleasure of taking the back seat. With the kind of smile they would give to the behavior of Margaret the wife in "Father Knows Best," they talked about the one assertion of Mary's recorded in the Gospel: her request at the wedding feast at Cana. It was noted that she didn't ask her son directly for anything; she merely said: "They have no wine." Making him think it was his decision. Not suggesting it was her idea, no, nothing like that. Then disappearing, once again into the background, into silence.

For women like her, Gordon said, it was necessary "to reject that image of Mary in order to hold onto the fragile hope of intellectual achievement, independence of identity, sexual fulfillment." She regretted that no alternative to this Marian image was offered. There were a few saints one could turn to such as Teresa of Avila, but "the appeal of Mary is that devotion to her is universal, ancient. And she is the mother of God."

Much of the thought about Mary, however, had been "poisoned by misogyny, and a hatred of the body, particularly female sexuality." The early Church Fathers did not like women, according to Gordon, and "in setting Mary apart from the rest of the female sex what they were saying was that she was only acceptable because she did not share the corruption that was inevitably attached to the female condition." The image of Mary as the second Eve had been present in Marian thought from the earliest times, and it was in talking about Eve that the early writers "gave vent to their disgust for sex and for female sexuality in general." Gordon quoted the early third-century theologian Tertullian: "Do you not realize, Eve, that it is you? The curse God pronounced on your sex weighs still on the world. Guiltily, you must bear its hardships. You are the devil's gateway, you desecrated the fatal tree, you first

betrayed the law of God, you softened up with your cajoling words the man against whom the devil could not prevail by force." She added other offensively misogynist quotations from Augustine, Jerome, Chrysostom, and others but said that she was determined to find more positive elements.

> I have wanted to create for myself a devotion to Mary that honors her as woman, as mother, that rejects the wickedness of sexual hatred and sexual fear. I wanted this particularly as I grew older; I longed for it with a special poignancy as I experienced motherhood for the first time. It has come to me, then, that one must sift through the nonsense and hostility that has characterized thought and writing about Mary, to find some images, shards, and fragments, glittering in the rubble. One must find isolated words, isolated images; one must travel the road of metaphor, of icon, to come back to that figure who, throughout a corrupt history, has moved the hearts of men and women, has triumphed over the hatred of women and fear of her, and abides shining, worthy of our love, compelling it.

Gordon then shared a creative meditation on the innocence, grief, and glory of Mary that drew on poetry, painting, sculpture, and music.[8]

Gordon's later novels and short stories, such as *Men and Angels* (1985) and *Temporary Shelter* (1986), continued to contain central figures that reflected "a kind of early imprinting with the form and habit of asking religious questions, so that they can never quiet them later, but only dull their sound or attempt to ignore it." That was the opinion of Rosemary Booth in a 1988 essay on Gordon, the first in a series of articles in *Commonweal* on contemporary Catholic writers of fiction.[9] Gordon's searching essay on Mary was an especially notable *Commonweal* entry.

Homosexuality and the Priesthood

The Reverend Richard P. McBrien, chairman of the theology department at the University of Notre Dame, was courageous when he accepted the invitation of the editors of *Commonweal* to see if he had "any ecclesial reflections" on the widely reported presence of gay priests and seminarians. McBrien's article in June 1987 followed a report in *Newsweek* in February of that year that estimated that 20 percent of U.S. Catholic priests were homosexual and that half of those were sexually active.[10] Homosexuality was not a new topic in the pages of *Commonweal.* In 1973, for example, an editorial entitled "The Homosexual and the Church" and two articles on the same topic in a single issue of *Commonweal* produced a significant dialogue. Only a few months before McBrien's article, *Commonweal* had published an open letter to Cardinal Bernardin by Stephen Elred entitled "Gay rights/gay plight" and Bernardin's response.[11] Still, one could understand McBrien's caution when he said, "I am sure this article will set a new *Commonweal* record for Most Question Marks; it contains by contrast very few answers."[12] These were, however, questions "that must be articulated and addressed, however haltingly." The alternative was to leave them "to gossip, to unexamined, closed-door decisions, or to policy by default." In all, McBrien listed thirteen paragraphs of questions, beginning with such queries as "How many priests and seminarians are gay?" and "How many of those are active homosexuals?" and including "If there is, in fact, a large body of gay priests in the United States, is there any relation between this phenomenon and the increasing visibility of child-molestation cases involving Catholic clergy?" He acknowledged that we didn't have the answers to most of the questions. Research had to be done, and some answers were simply beyond the capacity of ordinary research methods. The questions required the skills of sociologists, psychologists, historians, ethicists, moral theologians, biblical scholars, and ecclesiologists.

As an ecclesiologist, McBrien offered the following observations. First, ministry is always done for the sake of the church. In the earliest days of the church, the community discerned the charisms and human qualities of ministry in certain baptized individuals and then applied every legitimate pressure upon those designees. Today, it works in the opposite fashion. Young men and, frequently, older "second-career" men, simply decide they would like to become a priest, then apply and advance to ordination and a pastoral assignment.

It is no secret that at least some of these applicants are not attracted primarily by the work of the presbyterial ministry but by the status and freedom from the ordinary demands of life that ordained ministry has often conferred. Indeed, it is not inconceivable that the ordained priesthood is attractive to certain people precisely because it excludes marriage. To put it plainly: as long as the church requires celibacy for the ordained priesthood, the priesthood will always pose a particular attraction for gay men who are otherwise not drawn to ministry in general or presbyterial ministry in particular.

Second, McBrien stated that the evidence available "suggests that obligatory celibacy is the most significant negative factor in the recent decline in vocations to the presbyterial ministry." Celibacy could not be described as an essential requirement for effective presbyterial service, since the original apostles were married, as were priests and bishops for several centuries during the church's early years. He further cited that Catholic priests in other rites are married and that the Latin Rite church itself had recently admitted former Episcopal priests into the Catholic priesthood and allowed them to function as married priests. The church's continued resistance to any change in obligatory celibacy would, according to McBrien, accelerate the current trend of heterosexual men choosing not to consider the priesthood as a lifelong ministerial vocation.

The church will have to draw increasingly from the homosexual community for its priests and seminarians, whether it likes it or not, and whether it wants to admit it or not. And in a society where homosexuality continues to be stigmatized, the celibate priesthood can offer an esteemed and rewarding profession in which "unmarried and uninterested" status is self-explanatory and excites neither curiosity or suspicion.

Third, McBrien stated that the presbyterial ministry is sacramental not only in the sense of being a dispenser of sacraments but also in the sense that the priest, like the bishop, must embody the sacred realities that he deals with every day. The bishop says to the person being ordained: "Let the example of your life attract the followers of Christ, so that by work and action you may build up the house which is God's church." Could a gay priest fulfill such a mandate? McBrien answers, "In principle, why not?" Homosexuals don't choose their sexual predisposition. Those who are not sexually active and who otherwise have all the necessary charisms and skills for presbyterial ministry have as much "right" to present themselves for ordination as do heterosexual candidates. If active homosexuals, however, are admitted and retained in the presbyterial ministry, and if their behavior becomes known, then the principle of sacramentality is engaged. The actively gay priest "sends a morally mixed message to the church and the wider community, to say the least."

> We can't have it both ways. We cannot continue to denounce homosexual behavior in our official teachings and disciplinary decrees, and then adopt an inexplicitly lax approach to the scrutiny of candidates for admission to our seminaries and for ordination. And that, of course, "goes double" for candidates to the episcopacy. We cannot say one thing in our doctrinal statements and countenance something entirely opposed to them in our church leaders.

Fourth, McBrien pointed out that by itself the ordination of women would have no major impact on the phenomenon of gay priests and gay seminarians. Without a change in the discipline of obligatory celibacy, opening the priesthood to women could simply intensify the problem with a possible influx of lesbian priests and lesbian seminarians.

In his conclusion, McBrien said he agreed with the central finding of the study by Dean R. Hoge of the department of sociology at the Catholic University of America. In *The Future of Catholic Leadership: Responses to the Priest Shortage* (Sheed and Ward, 1987), Hoge maintained that the shortage of priests was an institutional problem, not a spiritual one and that it could be corrected by institutional means. At the top of McBrien's means list was the elimination of obligatory celibacy. He maintained that this would remove one of the primary motives for the resignation of priests from the active ministry, would expand the pool of potential candidates for the ordained priesthood, and would "help correct the public's longstanding and deeply rooted perception of the Catholic church as a religion that regards sex as a necessary evil." These three reasons for the repeal of obligatory celibacy existed quite apart from any questions raised about homosexuality and the clergy. But fifth, and finally, "such a repeal would remove all ambiguity from the vocational decisions of homosexuals. They would clearly choose the presbyterial ministry for the sake of the church, and not for what it might offer in terms of occupational respectability and freedom from social suspicion."

Many readers responded to McBrien's article, and, as a result, *Commonweal* published five pages of correspondence and a brief response and commentary by the author.[13] One respondent pointed out that the Apostolic Pro-Nuncio to the United States, Archbishop Pio Laghi, had "cited mandatory celibacy for Western-rite clergy as one of the non-discussable and non-debatable issues with Pope John Paul II." The respondent felt that McBrien's article had made it even more imperative that the current discipline of mandatory celibacy be debated openly, honestly, and fully. "Although many of us applaud the courage of our bishops in standing up to presidents, governors, and senators in their defense of peace, the poor, life, and justice, we'd be more edified if they fulfilled their episcopal ordination and periodically stood up to the pope in dialogue." Archbishop Roger Mahony, also a respondent, clearly saw no need for this. McBrien, he said, was "out of touch with local, pastoral realities." The "reality" of Mahony's archdiocese of Los Angeles was an "outstanding presbyterate" of "well-adjusted heterosexual men who love Christ and the church, men who give of themselves in fullest generosity to the service of their people." It was perhaps understandable that Mahony might wish to contribute a remark like this, but McBrien had not suggested that there were not good numbers of such priests. Less understandable was Mahony's dismissal of Dean R. Hoge's study of the shortage of priests before even reading it, especially after calling him "a fine religious sociologist at the Catholic University of America" for whose work he had a "deep respect." Hoge's work on this question was flawed, suggested Mahony, by his "purely scientific" approach. Mahony said, "I prefer to place my confidence in Christ's promise and his abiding presence among us. . . . I simply don't have the same confidence in sociological studies, popularity polls, and similar 'modern devices.' " Hoge's book, let it be said, expressed no lack of confidence in the abiding presence of Christ. Hoge did, however, suggest that projections indicating seriously reduced numbers of male celibate Roman Catholic clergy should not be quickly dismissed.[14] One correspondent accused McBrien of "homophobia" for his failure to put homosexual and heterosexual behavior on an equal moral basis, that is, allowing each to marry. Others, including Bishop Mahony, saw McBrien as presenting optional celibacy as a "panacea" for the problem of homosexuality in the priesthood. Concerning the alleged homophobia, McBrien said he had no intention of opening new ethical or doctrinal ground in the essay. In response to the "panacea" charge, McBrien stressed that he had not proposed a married clergy as a panacea for the homosexuality problem or any other. Catholic moral theologian John W. Glaser wrote that the article and its related questions needed more dialogue with the gay community. McBrien agreed but pointed out that such a dialogue would likely be more difficult "given some of our pastoral leaders' current determination to block even the celebration of the Eucharist for largely gay congregations."

The McBrien essay, and the dialogue that it produced, provided an unusual moment of candor on a topic that still needs attention. Whether that will happen is questionable. The forums for this are too few, and the potential participants too intimidated.

Commonweal Columnists

A review of *Commonweal* in the 1970s and 1980s would be incomplete without acknowledging its regular columnists. Peter Steinfels's contributions as a columnist during his years away from regular editorial duties have been mentioned, and the columns contributed by *Commonweal* stalwarts James O'Gara and John Cogley have been recalled. Michael Novak in the early 1970s and Frank Getlein in the later 1970s were notable columnists. Novak had been a *Commonweal* associate editor (at large) from 1967 to 1971. Getlein and other columnists, such as J. Bryan Hehir, contributed important periodic columns but held no editorial position with the magazine. The same is true for John Garvey and Abigail McCarthy, whose columns have been regular and appealing features to *Commonweal* readers from their inception in the mid-1970s.

John Garvey, an editor with Templegate Publishers in Springfield, Illinois, and author of *Saints for Confused Times* (Thomas More, 1986),[15] became a regular columnist in 1976. His 1979 essay on celibacy offers an example of his work that was regarded as particularly timely. "A Married Layman on Celibacy" challenged a cultural atmosphere that tended to regard vows as anachronisms.

> Vows are considered less than central to the business of being human today because of the individualism which pervades Western culture: unless something can be shown to be of obvious and more or less immediate benefit to the individual, its value is questioned. The vow challenges this mentality by suggesting that self-fulfillment and personal freedom, good as they are, are not only not enough to make for a good life; a life which sets them as goals is too small a life. As Christians we are called to something larger and stranger than the life the world offers us; we are called to a deeper life, which discloses itself during the course of our life and is fulfilled at death. This, anyway, is our hope, the risk we take, and our evidence, such as it is, is to be found in the lives of people who went before us and lived well.

A vow, whether of marriage or of celibacy, he maintained, can help call us out of ourselves to a larger life, to a participation in God's own life.

Garvey rejected some of the justifications of celibacy. He asserted that the argument of practicality and availability, that is, that the celibate is more available and more able to respond to those in need because he is not tied down to a wife or children was not convincing. "For one thing, I have yet to meet a celibate whose celibacy had directly to do with his availability. By this I don't mean that I haven't met genuinely generous celibates—I have. But they were not more generous than the generous doctors I have known, or the generous married couples whose homes have been havens for many people, whose lives are open to those in need at every moment." He also rejected the argument that the celibate, in committing his love to no particular person, is free to love everyone:

> This contradicts the experience of love by making it a rationed thing, as if having spent 75 litres of love on one's wife and children, one had only 25 litres of God's allotment left for the rest of the race. In fact by learning to love one other person deeply, one learns to love every other person that much more deeply. The love that a man and woman have for one another and for their children is, if it is Christian, carried into the rest of their lives and into every other relationship.

Garvey stressed that the paradoxical nature of celibacy should not be explained away or made to look like a practical and beneficial thing. He described the Christian tradition as proclaiming firmly that the world is good, that sex and procreation are good, and that pleasure well taken is loved by God and that it is only within the context of a refreshed sense of the ascetic that celibacy can make sense.

> Celibacy is a kind of fast. Like fasting from food and drink, like voluntary poverty, it makes no worldly sense. It makes sense only if God is real. Like fasting

and voluntary poverty, celibacy is a witness to a life which is more profoundly real than the life offered by the world. Celibacy has not worldly justification (and this is why practical, sensible arguments in its favor sell it short, just as the argument that fasting is good for the figure misses the point of fasting), but it makes sense in the context of the reality of God's kingdom.

Garvey noted that C. S. Lewis had pointed out that there is always a tendency to warn a people living in a particular time against the danger into which they are least likely to fall; so in a puritanical age, we are warned against licentiousness, and in a licentious age, we are warned against puritanism. It is not, said Garvey, a danger of asceticism that the Western world needs to fear in the late twentieth century. A freely chosen celibacy that exhibits the love it is based in and the paradoxical strength in weakness of which St. Paul boasts will have many moments of loneliness, but can be a powerful witness to the kingdom of God.[16]

Among the appreciative letters responding to the Garvey essay was one by theologian Robert Imbelli who called it "one of the finest short statements which I have read on an issue which seems to suffer as much from the rhetoric of its proponents as from the incomprehension of its opponents."[17]

In other columns Garvey touched on mandatory celibacy and noted its negative impact on the life of the contemporary church, regretting the Vatican's refusal of the request made by many missionary bishops for a married priesthood, "as if celibacy were more important than the right of baptized people to receive the Eucharist."[18] He also critiqued the routine denial of priests' requests for laicizations by Pope John Paul II.[19] The themes of Garvey's essays were generally concerns about religious meaning in life. He dealt with these in ways that sensitively engaged the broad and diverse readership of *Commonweal*. His essay "Family Photographs" ("A family photograph is about something which is in fact threatened, and at its best has virtues the culture does not encourage")[20] was of this nature. His 1977 essay, "Man Becomes God" was possibly the best Christmas essay since John

Cogley's "Every Christmas," in 1952, which was built around Cogley's recollections of a Christmas class play from his third grade days. Garvey wrote that the radicalism of the Incarnation might seem to have been domesticated by our tendency of celebrating Christmas simply as a jolly feast. Christmas was "a good time to reflect on what the Fathers of the church called *deification,* the belief that we are meant to share in divinity, and that anything less is less than Christianity."[21] The style was not Cogley's but the richness of thought was similar, as was the essence of what their essays mutually affirmed. In 1985, distinguished historian and longtime reader of *Commonweal* Monsignor John Tracy Ellis wrote to praise one of Garvey's essays and referred to him as "always worth reading."[22]

Abigail McCarthy began writing her column in *Commonweal* in April 1974. While Garvey could write—and did —of his experience of helping to prepare his son for confirmation,[23] McCarthy's context was that of a person of more mature years. A 1936 Phi Beta Kappa graduate from St. Catherine's College in St. Paul, she went on to pursue a master's degree from the University of Minnesota. She met Eugene McCarthy while both were teaching in Mandan, North Dakota. They married in 1945 and had four children. Her book *Private Faces/Public Places* (Doubleday, 1972), had a broad appeal for both men and women and was inadequately described on its book jacket as "a candid portrait of an American woman, of a marriage, and of some of the people and events that have shaped our time." It was, rather, a personal memoir of uncommon insight and wisdom, written with an elegantly graceful simplicity. McCarthy concluded the book with a remark about wanting to bring with her into the future "a sense of the past, its continuity into the present, and a sense of identity stemming from the past which enables each of us to withstand the assault of change."[24] This was written in the one-page epilogue, which reported the decision of her husband to leave her and their marriage in August 1969, a year after his well-known and historically significant campaign for president in 1968.

McCarthy proved to be a very durable and significant columnist for *Commonweal.* She was sensitive and attentive to questions regarding the status of women, pointing out "the tenacious obduracy to change in male dominated institutions." In "Don't Call Us, We'll Call You: What the Synod Said to Women," she spoke approvingly of Milwaukee Archbishop Rembert Weakland's call at the 1987 Synod on the Laity that women be allowed to serve fully in all nonordained ministries. "Not awfully bold at the end of the twentieth century," she commented, "but heartening." When this proposal was dismissed on the basis that cultural variations in the entire world had to be considered, she said it was "pretty hard to think of a late-twentieth-century culture (outside of the Ayatollah's) where representatives of the majority of the baptized serving in the sanctuary or pulpit would be too unsettling."[25]

In "Justice for Mothers: Reflections for the Annual Spring Ritual," she noted that "the annual national celebration of motherhood is pretty much a matter of lip service." She called for structural changes to relieve the problems of young mothers, older mothers, and widows.[26] McCarthy always held respect for those women whose career was that of wife and mother. In 1980, she wrote sympathetically of Barbara Bush's frustration with a reporter's persistent and repetitious questioning:

> What couldn't the interviewer understand? That Mrs. Bush had married young, had been married to the same man for thirty-four years, that she had no career other than wifehood, rearing her children and performing the civic and volunteer duties associated with marriage to a prominent man. And that, furthermore, she insisted that she was fulfilled by that career, and more, had grown and developed in capability and independence as a result of it.[27]

McCarthy pointed out that the role that Barbara Bush had accepted and enjoyed had been considered the ideal role that many women had aspired to and many continued to aspire to that role. McCarthy clearly had no desire to demean or diminish it.

McCarthy's interests were broad and included literary, social, and political commentary. If there was an overarching theme, it seemed to be the quest for a human and religious authenticity. Occasionally she wrote about sisters. In "The Spirit of Venantia: What Sister Really Said," she wrote as "a Catholic writer who does not remember the teaching sisters of my childhood as either blighted or blighting." She remembered Sister Venantia as a legendary name of her youth, who had taught both the generation of her grandparents and her parents. She had come with three other sisters to a young midwestern town, founded its parochial school, and set its traditions:

> The sisters who taught me were the true daughters of Venantia. Good solid teaching was the hallmark of their community—not for nothing called the School Sisters of Notre Dame—and they were enthusiastic teachers. Order was necessary for learning and they maintained it, but not once in twelve years did I see one of them resort to corporal punishment to do so. (It isn't that I don't believe those stories of vengeful nuns wielding rulers, it's just that they are only that to me—stories.) Our wrong-doers stayed after school, did extra homework, or wrote I-must-not-this-or-that fifty or one hundred times. The more obstreperous were summoned to sit on sister's platform or were banished to the cloakroom. Real villains got low marks in "deportment" and faced the roars of the pastor and the wrath and shame of their parents on report card day. Looking back I see now that social pressure was the key to order, and that the social climate had been created by Sister Venantia, a true women of the pioneers.

The sisters are fewer now, said McCarthy, and they have gone on to many more areas of service than education, but "the spirit of Venantia lives on now in their work in prisons, in inner cities, in Latin America."

> I don't think we should begrudge them this change. But in this season of fantasies like *Sister Mary Ignatius* and *Agnes of God* on the New York stage,

it seems a good time to pay tribute to the different, and real, sisters of my memory.[28]

In "The Nun's (Old) Story: Encountering Obstacles Is Nothing New," McCarthy commented on a 1983 letter by Pope John Paul II to U.S. bishops concerning religious orders. The letter called for a study headed by Archbishop John Quinn of San Francisco. Accompanying the pope's letter was a document on the "Essential Elements in Church Teaching and Religious Life" issued by the Vatican Congregation for Religious.[29] "It seems to be an unhappy fact," McCarthy opened her essay, "that our American sisters have been frightening churchmen in Rome half to death." Was Rome now conducting a study or an investigation? It was not certain, she said, that discovery was the real interest of the Vatican. There was in the pope's letter a sense of "going back" to big convents and the dress of the older habit. More fundamentally, many religious felt that their rightful autonomy and initiative in apostolic service was being threatened by the emphasis in the documents on a hierarchical model of ecclesiastical authority. To sisters and their friends who knew the history of religious communities, said McCarthy, this emphasis was threatening. She pointed out that it was two hundred years after the sisters adopted active rather than contemplative apostolates before Rome approved their doing so! Reviewing the enormous contribution sisters in active apostolates had made in America to preserving the faith of immigrant people from dozens of different countries and lifting them into the mainstream of American life, she commented: "Yet, if ecclesiastical authority had really held sway—if the bishops had been left to coordinate the church's energies, as the Pope puts it—none of the teaching sisters who did this work in the past would have been available. Their religious communities would not have existed." McCarthy commended the quiet persistence with which sisters who felt a calling to the active apostolate had found ways around the obstacles placed in their paths.

McCarthy speculated that the 1983 Rome-initiated study and instruction in "essentials" may have been stimulated by complaints from within the United States:

No doubt many misguided Americans have complained about our sisters. They should remember
that our sisters are neither pets nor children to be
taken out on yearly outings to circuses or ball
games and treated to ice cream and cotton candy.
They are mature women in a period of transition.

These women hear different calls, she stated, the most
compelling of which is "to be with the poor." Undoubtedly
they will make and have made mistakes, but "we must let
them find their own way. We owe them that."[30]

John Garvey, Abigail McCarthy, and the other columnists
contributed much to the vitality and wisdom of *Commonweal*
in the 1970s and 1980s.

5

The Papacy

It wasn't a negative attitude about Pope Paul VI that led
Commonweal to publish its editorial "Why the Pope Should
Resign" in November 1977. That summer, at eighty years of
age and after fourteen years as pope, the pope himself had
said, "I see the end of my life approaching." In October he
had offered to give himself as a hostage to gain the freedom
of eighty-six hostages held captive in a West German airliner
in Somalia. *Commonweal* noted that these actions indicated
"not only that he accepts death—since to become the hostage
of terrorists is virtually to invite martyrdom—but also that he
does not see his continued reign as indispensable to the
church." The pope had indirectly indicated that only he could
decide how long he should be pope. Further, he had already
required bishops to retire at seventy-five and had barred cardinals over eighty from voting in papal elections. The tempo-
ral nature of the papal office, *Commonweal* pointed out, was
both a theological truth and a historical fact. We have been
conditioned, however, to visualize a papacy "where the religious leader, like a king, endures, powers failing, to the last
hour, while courtiers jockey for his favor or his ear. We are
still stuck with a papacy modeled on European monarchy,

constructed to meet a real need for an independent and stable religious institution." That seemed to call for a lifetime term in a time when men didn't live quite so long. In the present democratic age it seemed rather "the reluctance of Roman curial officials to relinquish their power that has kept modern popes hanging on till death." Calling Paul VI "perhaps the most intelligent of modern popes," they said that he knew he was neither an emperor nor a king but "a servant—like Christ, the servant of servants"—and one who profoundly understood the power of a symbolic act. He should retire, the editors believed, because the picture of a pope who has enough confidence that he need not maintain control until death will communicate "a more vigorous, credible, realistic, humble and hopeful message about the church."[1]

The Year of Three Popes

A year later, both Paul VI and his successor, Pope John Paul I, Albino Luciani, were dead. Luciani, who had served as Patriarch of Venice, died after only thirty-four days as pope. Church historian Father John Jay Hughes asked in *Commonweal* whether the church was well served by a system that excluded from serious consideration for its highest office candidates younger than sixty? "Where but in the Catholic Church would men in their late fifties be considered 'too young' for election to one of the world's most onerous positions?" Discussion had been limited, he said, to speculation about applying the present age limit of seventy-five for bishops to the Bishop of Rome. Hughes offered another approach: the election of a pope for a fixed term. What about ten years?, he suggested. Hughes acknowledged that only a pope could change the regulations in such a matter, but since the ten-year rule was already followed by superiors of most religious orders it seemed worthy of consideration. It would be "quite long enough to permit a pope to set his stamp upon the church, without killing him in the process. It would open the church's highest office to men in their prime not only at their election, but with the additional promise of continued vigor at the conclusion of their term."[2]

On October 16, 1978, Karol Wojtyla, at age fifty-eight, became the first Slavic pope and the first non-Italian since

1523. As Peter Hebblethwaite remarked in his account of the October conclave, "After the sudden death of the pope and in view of the intolerable demands of the office, a younger man—someone in his fifties—could now be contemplated with equanimity and relief."[3] He was elected, apparently on the eighth ballot, when no consensus was found for any Italian candidate. Almost all observers failed to see Cardinal Wojtyla as a possible pope, says Hebblethwaite, because they "simply underestimated the courage and imagination of the College of Cardinals."[4]

John Jay Hughes enthusiastically wrote in *Commonweal* that "the church's need for vigorous, fresh leadership in a time of crisis had been recognized and met." The selection of a non-Italian would help diminish the papacy's "entanglement in numerous no-win Italian political controversies" and would complete "the spiritual liberation of the papacy which began with the loss of the Papal States over a century ago." With imagination and charm Wojtyla had won the Italian crowd in his first appearance on the loggia of St. Peter's. *"Sia lodato Gesu Cristo"* ("Praised be Jesus Christ"). With these words, spoken in flawless Italian, the first non-Italian pope in 455 years presented himself to the members of his local church and, by television, to the world. He spoke to them simply and informally in Italian and asked them to "correct me, if I make mistakes in your—in our—language." Hughes saw the new pope as pledged to the expansion of collegiality, having a demonstrated interest in ecumenism, and enjoying the benefit of being heir to the Paul VI reform of the curia. Paul had eliminated the permanent appointments of top officials in "the world's oldest functioning bureaucracy" that had allowed them to boast that "Popes come and go, but the curia remains forever." Top curial appointments were now for five years and lapsed with the pope's death. Paul had also made the College of Cardinals far more representative of the international church. A majority of the voting cardinals were now non-Europeans, and over a third came from Third World countries. Believing that these changes made the surprising election possible, Hughes said that "history may yet record the choice of Karol Wojtyla as Paul VI's greatest achievement."

In the midst of "all the euphoria and rejoicing," Hughes did not wish to conceal some misgivings. "Catholics who in the

United States call themselves liberal (elsewhere we are termed progressive) fear the new Pope's future decisions, especially with regard to such questions as clerical celibacy, contraception, the ordination of women, and the readmission to the sacraments of invalidly married Catholics."[5] Distinguished historian Monsignor John Tracy Ellis wrote in praise of the Hughes article and said he suspected that the author's final list of misgivings "may prove in the time ahead to have been solidly based." Ellis felt that "John Paul II may offer the latest example of a long line of churchmen who have been socially progressive and at the same time theologically conservative."[6] Meanwhile, *Commonweal* hoped that the new and vigorous papal witness of John Paul II might help "an unbelieving and half believing world look for ultimate meaning beyond itself."[7]

John Paul II in the U.S.

Pope John Paul II's visit to the United States in October 1979 found *Commonweal* speaking of the "cascade of dramatic moments" in the tour and of the pope's "extraordinary personal magnetism." A key question, however, was how this charisma would be translated into leadership. The editors had particular praise for the pope's speech to the United Nations with its "careful explication of the interrelationship between spiritual and material rights." They were "deeply troubled," however, by the papal statements directed essentially at Catholics:

> The pope dealt with a range of issues, often in a swift and assertive manner. Each of them deserves consideration in its own right. The release of priests from their vows, for example, is not the same issue as the future of the celibate priesthood in the Roman rite. Abortion, homosexuality and contraception are separate questions—and the pope has probably contributed to the difficulties already existing in the public debate by appearing to treat them as a piece. Whether the ordination of women poses a question of human rights depends entirely on the grounds for disallowing such ordination. Unless the church pre-

sents better reasons against such ordination than have so far been adduced, it is hard to see why human rights are not pertinent any less than if the priesthood were denied to members of certain races or if the church revived its traditional teachings on slavery.

Commonweal felt that it was not so much the specific positions taken by the pope but rather his vision of the teaching church that gave them the most concern. Repeatedly, the pope invoked the image of the "deposit of truth" to be safeguarded and effectively communicated "as though it were a static, reified reality, a treasure protected and at most given a different display case for every age, rather than a living and growing tradition rooted in history and experience." The validity of the Christian testimony of masses of believers and of disparate local churches seemed to be affirmed "only when it matched the view from the top." The pope's insistence on human rights in his addresses on the secular order found little echo in his statements essentially to Catholics. Instead, these statements to Catholics seemed to feature a dismissal of such rights—especially in connection with women's ordination—and a declaration of "the right of the faithful not to be troubled by theories and hypotheses that they are not expert in judging or that are easily simplified or manipulated by public opinion for ends that are alien to the truth." In an age of fads and media oversimplification, said *Commonweal*, it was "not hard to divine some truth in a phrase about 'the right . . . , not to be troubled,' but if such a phrase had a ring that seemed more fitting to the Polish communist party rather than to a dissenting Polish religious leader, it was because the institutional behavior based on such phrases more commonly resembled that of authoritarian societies than communities of free and mature believers."

Commonweal discerned that the characteristic note of the pope's personal appearances was "a loving openness to human cares and experience." If his words, however, were taken as approval of closed and authoritarian church institutions, then the link between charisma and leadership would be lost. "A pilgrimage that was magnificently inclusive will reinforce what, in the church, is militantly exclusive."

They felt that the pope was trying to articulate "his particular heroic vision of the church."

> That Christ must be central, that love is demanding, that faithfulness requires sacrifice, that drift should be resisted—this should be readily endorsed, however hard to live by. But insofar as his vision minimizes the continuing struggle not only to communicate old truths effectively but, in the light of experience, really discover what the old truths mean; insofar as it encourages a teaching church that is not equally a learning one, the huge promise of his papacy may go unfulfilled.[8]

The New Inquisition?

Saturday, December 15, 1979, was, said Peter Hebblethwaite, "a day to remember in the life of the Roman Catholic Church—though theologians may prefer to forget it." On this day, the Congregation for the Doctrine of the Faith (CDF) conducted a meeting investigating the orthodoxy of Father Edward Schillebeeckx, O.P., while elsewhere in the same building, the Prefect of the CDF, signed a declaration designed to end the career of Father Hans Küng as a Roman Catholic theologian. That evening Pope John Paul II delivered an address at the Gregorian University in Rome on the role of theologians in the church. "A single day, then, that changed the Church, just before Christmas," wrote Hebblethwaite.[9]

Commonweal's editorial lamented that the institutional church was on a collision course with its intellectuals and suggested that actions against such distinguished theologians, both of whom were theological *periti* or experts at Vatican II, gave the appearance that Rome feared rather than promoted the "quest for truth."[10]

Hebblethwaite saw "the new policy towards theologians" as fitting in with John Paul's zest to "tackle problems head on."

> He does not beat about the bush. Where Paul VI was cautious, dilatory, diplomatic and reluctant to

provoke an open break, John Paul II charges dashingly ahead like the Polish cavalry, in pursuit of his vision of a Church in which order will have been restored. At the Vatican Council, Paul VI always sought for compromise which meant that, as he put it, there would be *pas de vaincus, mais des convaincus* (no vanquished but only the convinced). John Paul II does not seem to mind if the battlefield is strewn with the corpses of fallen theologians.[11]

The "cavalry charge" continued throughout the 1980s, as did the casualty list that included theologians from around the world as well as some sisters and bishops.

Commonweal's 1984 editorial "Polarization in the Church?" found an atmosphere of internal tension in the church that was "not healthy." The immediate situation involved an initiative by the Congregation for the Doctrine of the Faith, headed by Cardinal Ratzinger, against Latin American liberation theology, specifically Peru's Gustavo Gutiérrez and El Salvador's Jon Sobrino. Gutiérrez and Sobrino were accused of undermining hierarchical authority and fomenting class war. The CDF also withdrew the imprimatur (permission to publish) from two books published by Paulist Press in the United States, the widely read adult catechism *Christ Among Us* by Anthony T. Wilhelm and *Sexual Morality* by the Sulpician priest, Father Philip S. Keane. *Commonweal* was astounded by the suppression of the Paulist books—"no prior consultation with authors or publisher, no due process for sullied reputations, no effort to explain objections, the bishops who originally gave the imprimaturs demeaned as messenger boys." All this was "breathtaking" for its lack of regard for decency of process. Furthermore, collegiality was "shrunk like Alice to pin size." Such authoritarian responses to disputed questions, they warned, are counterproductive and discredit authority:

> Party lines harden. Fears of arbitrary Vatican actions inhibit candid criticism and thoroughgoing discussion of controversial authors or lines of thought that are under fire from Rome. . . . Polemic breeds

sourness and self-righteousness, of which there is already too much in the church.

Commonweal noted that in matters of internal church discipline the vigor and vision of John Paul II "seemed either to yield to the practices of the Vatican bureaucrats or, in fact, to run strongly against the more decentralized, pluralistic kind of church which had ignited the vitality that, in other respects, the new pope eloquently communicated to the world."[12]

Some Protestant Views

Albert Outler, the distinguished Methodist theologian who was an official observer at Vatican II, wrote praising the editorial as "clear, firm—and civil." John Paul II, he stated, "is a gracious, open-hearted man and many of his visions are heart-lifting (e.g., distributive justice); but his idea of Christian unity seems to be the return of the rest of us to the Roman communion, made as cordial and hospitable as possible." The Secretariat for Promoting Christian Unity, said Outler, "used to be an anteroom to the Apostolic Palace; now it is barely hanging on down there on the Via dei Corridori." He regretted that many Catholics in high places were reading the decree on ecumenism "in as conservative a way as the text allows." He acknowledged that there were also lapses and forfeited opportunities on the part of Protestants, adding that "many of the Christian people are a good way ahead of many of their leaders."[13]

Early in the papacy of John Paul II, Stanley Hauerwas and Robert Wilken, Protestant professors of theology at Notre Dame, wrote in *Commonweal* of their hope that the pope would "realize he has a ministry which is not confined to the Roman Catholic church but to all Christians." They reported, however, that his first visit to the United States was less than satisfying to many Protestants. "It was as if the pope had set out to reconfirm our past stereotypes of the papacy and to reawaken feelings that we thought were long forgotten." A specific grievance was John Paul II's repeated use of the term "Vicar of Christ" to apply to himself.

As far as we are aware this title has dropped out of papal speeches in recent years, and its appearance gave us pause. . . . Modern historical scholarship has confirmed that the term Vicar of Christ did not become a title for the pope until the middle ages, and that it was not until the thirteenth century during the papacy of Innocent III (1189–1219), that it became the exclusive title of the pope, superseding earlier titles such as Vicar of St. Peter. Innocent III envisioned himself as a priest-king, an intermediary between God and man, the locus of divine authority in the world, the source from which the political authority derived its power as the "moon derives her light from the sun."

The history, as sketched by Hauerwas and Wilken, is indeed sustained by such modern Catholic scholars as Father J. M. R. Tillard, O.P., in *The Bishop of Rome* (Michael Glazier, 1983). In their *Commonweal* article, Hauerwas and Wilken stated that in singling out the title "Vicar of Christ" and recalling its historical significance, they were not implying that John Paul II imagined himself a latter-day Innocent III, nor that the title had in the pope's mind the meaning it presumably had for medieval or Renaissance popes. "What we do wish to say, however, is that the title does reawaken an imperialist, even divine view, of the papacy, and that it denies the ecclesial reality of the separated churches."[14] They felt that John Paul II and many Catholics needed to be reminded how offensive such language was to Christians who belong to the Protestant and Orthodox churches.

Another distinguished Protestant scholar, Richard John Neuhaus, on the other hand, spoke in rather unreserved praise of Pope John Paul II. He felt that under this pope, Catholicism was "more fully Catholic as it is less hesitantly Roman." Neuhaus noted too the significance that both John Paul I and John Paul II had been *installed*—not crowned—and he was much impressed not only by the official setting aside of the papal tiara but also by papal leadership in dealing with the modern crisis of unbelief. As Neuhaus saw it, the major work of the pope was his "attempting to chart a

Christian course that is not so much against modernity as it is beyond modernity." The only modernity that needed to be discarded, said Neuhaus, was "the debased modernity of unbelief that results in a prideful and premature closure of the world against its promised destiny." The Lutheran scholar and pastor proclaimed that while it was said that Pope John XXIII opened the windows of the church to the modern world, John Paul II had "entered the modern world to help open the windows of the modern world to the worlds of which it is part."[15]

The Shooting of the Pope

When the pope was shot by Mehmet Ali Agca in 1981, *Commonweal* spoke of John Paul II's "near universal appeal, even when one disagrees with some of his statements" and noted also the influence of the pope as a master ritualist whose "genuinely charismatic presence in those vast public liturgies seemed to address some great repressed need in countless numbers of people, many of them non-Catholic." *Commonweal* was grateful that the dramatic and touching influence of what they approvingly called the "papal theater" had not been extinguished by Agca's bullets.[16]

Three years later, the pope's visit to the cell of Agca caught the world's imagination, prompting *Time* magazine, for example, to publish a rather unusual cover story on forgiveness. In the course of its story *Time* pointed out that if you could have pulled back far enough on that striking picture of pope and assassin hunched together, you would have seen a still photographer and a television crew, all arranged by the Vatican. *Commonweal* acknowledged that the pope did not "leave his media coverage to chance," but noted, in his defense, that if he were not "a master of the media," then no one, neither *Time* nor *Commonweal*, would have been provoked into writing and reflecting about reconciliation. For *Commonweal*, the reflection included a vision of reconciliation that challenged themselves in their relationship with Michael Novak (more on that later) and of a grand gathering that might have included John Paul, Hans Küng, alienated Catholic women, and others.[17]

A World Perspective

Asked to appraise John Paul II in an interview, *Commonweal* editor Peter Steinfels pointed out that although we talk about a world church, we tend to forget the reality that the pope deals with at least three worlds: first, the advanced postindustrial societies of the West; second, the communist world; and third, the developing countries. "It may be that the same pope is not a great pope for all three worlds at the same time," Steinfels said. He felt that the pope had been wonderful in dealing with the communist world and perhaps also, in the long run, in dealing with the developing countries of the Third World. He was, however, noted Steinfels, missing opportunities to deal with major problems regarding women and sexuality in the First World. "To the extent that I think these questions are eventually going to face those other two worlds, I think it's a real shame that a pope as vigorous and intellectually compelling and spiritually compelling as this one, is not dealing with these," he said. And maybe, Steinfels added, the church won't get "another good chance" at these issues.[18]

A Celebration of Hope and Meaning

At the time of the pope's second visit to the United States, in 1987, *Commonweal* commented on the media's preoccupation with what was variously called "pick-and-choose Catholicism," "cafeteria Catholicism," or "smorgasbord Catholicism." Such labels, *Commonweal* felt, vastly exaggerated the disagreements American Catholics had with official church teachings. "By and large, Catholics are not picking a random four of the seven sacraments, six of the Ten Commandments, and three out of four Gospels," the magazine said. These much publicized disagreements , though significant, deal only with "a relatively, restricted and specific set of church positions, primarily related to sex, marriage and the treatment of women." *Commonweal* believed rather that the more important story was the striking demonstration of commitments of faith and hope. "During the papal visit, millions of Catholics have been affirming their belief that, despite the suffering and cruelty witnessed on every side, this universe is created and sustained by a God of love, who in Jesus Christ, has joined the human journey and promises victory over death, and whose Spirit enlivens us daily in the church's words and sacraments. In an age that often thinks itself secular, such a massive affirmation shouldn't be taken for granted—nor overshadowed by a difference over birth control."[19]

6

The Challenge of Peace

Peter Steinfels expressed the general editorial viewpoint at *Commonweal* when he spoke of a preference to see the magazine deal more with broadly religious as well as religion and society issues rather than church questions. At times, a particular church issue—mandatory clerical celibacy, for example—may, however, have taken on more presence in the magazine than it would have simply because *Commonweal* was one of the few platforms in which such a topic might be discussed. He regreted the polarization that he felt was forced by Rome in the 1980s and found the succession of internal church battles "dispiriting." He sensed a stabilizing atmosphere emerging within the Catholic church in the United States from the mid-1970s on, and both he and the magazine wanted to explore the creative possibilities that such a stable environment could provide to "guide that, foster that, not let it get sidelined."[1] We discussed earlier the memo Steinfels wrote upon assuming the editorship of *Commonweal*, a memo that expressed in detail these kinds of goals for the magazine.

For all these reasons, *Commonweal* welcomed the initiatives and the process from 1980 to 1983 that resulted in the pastoral letter *The Challenge of Peace: God's Promise and Our*

Response of the National Conference of Catholic Bishops.[2] Distinguished historian Monsignor John Tracy Ellis has stated: "Not only did the pastoral letter take positions contrary to those of many in high government circles . . . but what likewise distinguished the document was the unprecedented consultation that preceded its publication. In itself that process provided revealing evidence of the maturity gained by American Catholics, vis-à-vis their own coreligionists and as well the American public in general."[3] The process included the public circulation of three successive drafts of the document and a long list of highly qualified witnesses who appeared before the drafting committee. Secretary of Defense Caspar Weinberger and two of his predecessors, a variety of military, government, and arms control specialists as well as Protestant and Catholic theologians and ethicists and peace activists contributed testimony.[4] George F. Kennan, whom James Reston of the *New York Times* has described as "probably our most thoughtful and experienced foreign policy philosopher," has called the pastoral letter "the most profound and searching inquiry yet conducted by any responsible collective body into the relations of nuclear weaponry, and indeed of modern war in general, to moral philosophy, to politics and to the conscience of the national state."[5]

Commonweal contributed to the process that produced the pastoral letter by soliciting responses to the first draft from nine individuals who offered a range of viewpoints and a breadth of experience in confronting questions of peace and war.[6] Later, the magazine expressed "much admiration" for the second draft. On the key question of deterrence, *Commonweal* supported the view that the possession of nuclear arms for deterrence was "morally acceptable, not as an end in itself but as a step on the way toward progressive disarmament." *Commonweal* noted its view was in disagreement with "many of our pacifist friends at the *Catholic Worker* or *Sojourners* or even at the *National Catholic Reporter*."[7] *Commonweal* has long appreciated and respected pacifism, while not choosing it as its own view. It has, in short, supported and practiced a serious and critical use of the just-war tradition.[8] Four years after the publication of *The Challenge of Peace* in 1983, Peter Steinfels's continued commitment to nuclear deterrence prompted an unusual and public editorial dissent by assistant editor Patrick Jordan. *Commonweal's* editorial, said Jordan, erred in maintaining that the logical conclusion of rejecting nuclear deterrence was total and unilateral disarmament. Such a view, according to Jordan, was too pessimistic regarding the possibilities of multilateral, verifiable, and gradual reductions. This was a friendly but quite principled internal *Commonweal* debate, which appropriately found expression in its pages.[9]

Commonweal was pleased with the tone and style of *The Challenge of Peace*. The editors praised the bishops' statement, "This pastoral letter is more an invitation to continue the new appraisal of war and peace than a final synthesis." They found the bishops "far more humble in the face of their task than a good many of their critics."[10]

Commonweal regarded the third and final draft as "a wise and challenging guide for the church's peacemaking effort, and a serious contribution to the national search for a way back from the brink of nuclear catastrophe."[11]

The Challenge of Peace clearly opposed any first use of nuclear weapons, something NATO policy in Western Europe had reserved the right to, if necessary. It also opposed any use of nuclear weapons whatsoever against civilian populations or against military targets too close to concentrations of civilians. It repeated very strongly the statement of Vatican II: "Any act of war aimed indiscriminately at the destruction of entire cities or of extensive areas along with their population is a crime against God and man itself. It merits unequivocal and unhesitating condemnation."[12] The indictment against using nuclear weapons in a civilian setting had been made before—in 1968. But now this statement, and others like it, generated quite an impact. The television and print media reported extensively on the document, and cover stories appeared in the national newsweeklies.

Gerald P. Fogarty published an article in *Commonweal* entitled "Why the Pastoral Is Shocking" with the following subtitle: "Not Afraid to Challenge Government Policy." Fogarty, a Jesuit historian teaching at the University of Virginia, explained the significance of *The Challenge of Peace* in the context of the historical evolution of Catholicism as an integral part of American society. Catholicism had long been privatized: by its colonial suspect minority status, by the nativist reaction to its immigrant expansion, and by its attempts through service in successive wars to prove its Americanness. The order of the day, said Fogarty, was "private" religion, an interpretation that felt that the separation of church and state meant a divorce between religious belief and public policy. Change only came "when Catholics felt comfortable enough in being American that they no longer felt it necessary to prove their patriotism by uncritically accepting the nation's foreign policies and by serving in the armed forces." The present-day bishops, said Fogarty, were no longer afraid of being called un-American if they challenged governmental policy. Most were elevated to the episcopacy "after the cold war between Catholics and other Americans was ended." While the majority had not actually participated in Vatican II, all were nurtured in that council's teaching that the church is immersed in the world and thus "has a duty at times to criticize governments."[13]

This kind of participation by Catholics—and by all citizens—in society was something that *Commonweal* had upheld since its first issue in 1924. Indeed, such a communal attitude is inherent in the very name of the journal and was clearly a welcome development in the life of Catholicism in the United States.

7

Economics, Michael Novak, and *Economic Justice for All*

Commonweal has always regarded economics as important because if one cares about one's neighbors one must also care about the impact of the economy on one's neighbors. From its conception in 1924 to the present, therefore, the magazine has addressed economic issues, but never more notably nor more vigorously than in the 1980s.

One aspect of this economic interest is found in Peter Steinfels's lengthy two-part article on "Michael Novak and His Ultrasuper Democraticapitalism."[1] Novak was a *Commonweal* associate editor (at large) from 1967 to 1971 and a former *Commonweal* columnist, as was Steinfels in the 1970s. The titles of three of Novak's many books indicate phases in his personal evolution: *The Open Church* (Macmillan, 1964), *A Theology for Radical Politics* (Herder and Herder, 1969), and *The Rise of the Unmeltable Ethnics* (Macmillan, 1972). Novak, a Vatican II progressive, radicalized through the late 1960s, reaffirmed his Slavic ethnic origins. In the late 1970s, Novak became much more conservative, both ecclesiastically and politically, though he defined himself as a "neoliberal" and a

Democrat.[2] In 1982, with Ralph McInerny of Notre Dame, he founded a *Commonweal* look-alike called *Catholicism in Crisis*, later simply *Crisis*. He and McInerny were both dissatisfied with *Commonweal* and *America,* the Jesuit weekly, and as McInerny put it, "Novak's notion seemed the obvious solution. If you can't join 'em, lick 'em."[3] Both Novak and McInerny have, in fact, continued to write occasionally in *Commonweal*. In an interview, McInerny commented that *Crisis*'s promotional approaches that emphasized an alleged battle with *Commonweal* were "mostly hype."[4] Novak and McInerny's initial goal was to publish their first issue to coincide with and critique the draft of the bishops' letter *The Challenge of Peace*. They feared the view expressed in the letter, which was, in their mind, a wrong view would be taken as the only view one could offer from the Catholic tradition. Novak's lengthy essay "Moral Clarity in a Nuclear Age," which presented a differing Catholic view to that of the bishops, was so admired in *Crisis* by William F. Buckley that he reprinted it in its entirety, devoting an entire issue of the *National Review* to it.[5]

The overall crisis, however—as *Crisis* perceived it—was "the loss of the Catholic mentality" and its consequence: "a rampant relativism [that] goes uncorrected by epistemological and moral realism."[6] The most consistent concern in the pages of *Crisis* has proven to be contraception. McInerny, who supported *Humanae Vitae*, the 1968 papal encyclical against contraception, has stated that even if he didn't find the argument cogent, he would not disagree because it was proclaimed by "the Bishop of Rome, Christ's Vicar on Earth, and what they teach is what has always been taught."[7] Novak, who dissented vocally with the encyclical in 1968,[8] recanted his opposition in June 1989 in *Crisis,* saying "my obligation to the Holy See is to trust the Holy Spirit speaking through his legitimate voice."[9]

Steinfels's lengthy article in *Commonweal* focused on Novak's *The Spirit of Democratic Capitalism* (Simon and Schuster, 1982), but analyzed it within the corpus of Novak's writing. While documenting the remarkable shifts in Novak's views, something Novak himself had done in some measure in the book, Steinfels said it would be unfair to attribute Novak's changing opinions to fashion or opportunism, but asked why readers should be convinced that Novak's later views were any sounder that his earlier ones, especially since each new cause was "taken up with the same lack of restraint, the same sense that Michael Novak is the first to touch these shores, the same need to bolster his latest enthusiasm with the severest judgments on those whose outlook he had sympathetically portrayed not long before." In his critique, Steinfels found flaws in Novak's tendency to take anything beneficial connected with capitalism, for example, the material progress of Europe since 1800, and attribute it to democratic capitalism regardless of whether democracy was involved at all. Further, Novak had ignored a genuine historical link between capitalism and democracy in the eighteenth and early nineteenth century, namely liberalism, "which for some reason Novak has preferred not to name." Steinfels said that since the latter part of the nineteenth century, there was scarcely any expression of democratic reform toward which most capitalist leaders were not "at best, indifferent or, more commonly, hostile." He also faulted Novak's remark concerning German socialists in 1933, "only ninety-six of whom voted against the grant of dictatorial powers to Hitler." Steinfels explained, however, that this number constituted every possible socialist vote. "But if Novak cannot be expected to know that every single available socialist vote was cast against dictatorial powers for Hitler, he cannot be expected to know that every single vote of the German parties representing capitalism—and of the Catholic party too—was cast *for* Hitler's Enabling Act. Which, it seems, would be a more relevant topic of concern for an advocate of democratic capitalism to reflect upon."[10]

Novak maintained that democratic capitalism is characterized by three dynamic and converging systems functioning as one: a democratic polity, a capitalist economy based on markets and incentives, and a pluralistic moral cultural system and that these independent systems are at once balancing and sustaining.[11] Steinfels pointed out that sociologist Daniel Bell, who influenced Novak, used a similar tripartite framework of economy, polity, and culture as a *descriptive* framework for analyzing not capitalism but contemporary *society.* Steinfels maintained that Novak had turned Bell's descriptive framework into a normative one. Further, Novak had ignored one of Bell's own conclusions about the relationship of the realms:

"Though capitalism and democracy historically have arisen together, and have been commonly justified by philosophical liberalism, there is nothing which makes it either theoretically or practically necessary for the two to be yoked."[12]

Steinfels felt that Novak had always seen himself as speaking for the inarticulate underdog, "first student radicals, then ethnics, and now the Fortune 500. However implausible an 'underdog' the latter may seem . . . I think that Novak's excesses in *all* these causes have their roots in his belief that he is representing neither himself nor the truth but some inarticulate group that deserves its day in court."[13]

Steinfels warned that those who would gloat over the weaknesses found in Novak's book should "face the fact that the same faults abound in the political literature of the religious left."[14] The lack of precision, the neglect of carefulness in handling arguments of opposing theorists, and the absence of a genuine, historical sense were particular faults he noted.

Philosopher Bernard Murchland wrote *Commonweal* to say that Steinfels had read Novak "too narrowly through historical lenses" but it was true that Novak projected "democratic capitalism" too loosely over a long span of time and thus made himself vulnerable to criticism. Steinfels, however, had missed, according to Murchland, the book's creative exploration of the moral and theological basis upon which democratic capitalism rested. Mary Ash, a *Commonweal* letter writer, argued that *Commonweal*'s editorials indicated an "attraction for democratic socialism, although it often takes the guise of favoring substantial political intervention in the economy, while condemning capitalism as selfish and immoral." Novak, she said, had demonstrated that Catholic social teaching that supported this view rested on misunderstandings and warranted reassessment. Robert Benne, whose *Ethic of Democratic Capitalism* was reviewed critically but more favorably in the Steinfels article, said he appreciated "the fair and careful treatment" of his book.[15]

Novak felt rather differently. The article, he said, had an "immoderation" and "basic unfairness" about it "the like of which I can never remember seeing in *Commonweal*."[16] In terms of *Commonweal*'s long tradition of civility, Novak may have a legitimate grievance. A line such as, "I understand, therefore, the impulse not to take Novak seriously; indeed, the more I read him the more I understand it" would typically have been excised from a *Commonweal* article as a gratuitous slur.[17] Likewise, the title ("Michael Novak and His Ultrasuper Democraticapitalism") and the subtitle on the cover ("The Man Who Raised Amnesia to a Theological Principle") were immoderate as was the subtitle above the article itself ("The Unmeltable Ethnic Melts Down"). Murchland said he found venomous elements and "some ritualistic dumping on Novak" in the article but also "some confessional humility." Steinfels later said that he regretted that correspondents found anything venomous or unfair in the article and explained that he had wanted to deal extensively and seriously with the arguments Novak had raised.[18] Although there were some ill-chosen trappings to the article and some *ad hominem* one-liners that would better have been dropped, it was a serious and substantive piece. Also, the article's twelve-page length plus the six pages of correspondence may make it the most extensive treatment given any book in *Commonweal* history.

Commonweal was not the only journal raising questions about Novak's book, however. Reviewers in publications as varied as the *National Review* and the *New Republic* raised serious questions. Charles Krauthammer, like Steinfels, questioned a perhaps too simple assumption of balance in Novak's trinitarian system.

> What if, as George Will complains, the moral cultural system, far from being able to shoulder the responsibility for soulcraft, is itself leveled by capitalism's continuous revolution? What if, as Daniel Bell claimed, it is not an accident but a necessary consequence of the cultural contradictions of capitalism that it is undone by its own successes, that its abundance produces corruption and decay, that the constant change it engenders undermines the very traditional structures and values on which it depends?[19]

James Hitchcock, in the *National Review*, noted that occasionally Novak's rhetoric "gives off a whiff of the convert and the enthusiast" and that "he even seems at times to be singing a hymn of praise to the spiritual vacuum which exists at the heart of modern society." In places, he found the book "exhilarating," but by the time he finished, "alarm bells were going off all over my mind."[20] Michael Kerlin in *America* found aspects of Novak's argument "too contentious," but he accepted the basic idea of democratic capitalism and said the most significant debate should focus on what shape democratic capitalism should take and, above all, what balance should exist among the political, cultural, and economic systems.[21]

Economic Justice for All

By the end of the exchange between Steinfels and Novak in *Commonweal*, Michael Novak was emphasizing that his vision of democratic capitalism was not laissez-faire economics and that he indeed affirmed "the right and duty of the political system, and even more of the moral cultural system, to modify and to check the economic system."[22] (This theme, however, was not notably stressed in *The Spirit of Democratic Capitalism*). And in Steinfels's concluding remarks, he said that he was committed to reform rather than rejection of the existing capitalist system.[23] In principle, then, the two men agreed, though they would likely differ on the application of such a principle to the reform of the economic structure. Both were committed to the mission of making the existing economic order function in the most authentically serving way for the community.[24]

Novak and Steinfels had been the first people to appear before the committee of the National Conference of Catholic Bishops (NCCB), which had been appointed in 1980 to draft a pastoral letter on the U.S. economy. The same open process of hearings and public draft copies that occurred during the preparation of *The Challenge of Peace* was followed with this economics pastoral. Representatives from government, labor, and business, as well as farmers, economists, and Protestant, Catholic, and Jewish ethicists and theologians—more than one hundred men and women—contributed their insights.[25]

The first draft of *Economic Justice for All: Catholic Social Teaching and the U.S. Economy* appeared after the general election in November 1984[26] and followed the issuance of *Toward the Future: A Lay Letter on Catholic Social Thought and the U.S. Economy.*[27] "Rightist Catholics Pounce Before Hierarchy Speaks," said the *National Catholic Reporter* of this lengthy document, which was chiefly drafted by Michael Novak.[28] Novak had not only been the first person to speak before the NCCB committee but had been extended the courtesy of two additional appearances before the bishops' own drafting group. Novak was joined by thirty colleagues of a similar mind-set during the production phase of *Toward the Future.* One hundred thousand dollars was invested to hold hearings somewhat similar to those of the bishops' committee. *Commonweal* had modest praise for some elements of the "preemptive letter" but felt that it mostly reflected Novak's writings. The editors particularly faulted a press release from the Novak people who claimed it was "a representative group of lay Catholics."[29] Novak and James Finn, a former *Commonweal* editor and collaborator on the project, wrote defending the group authorship and its representative character. *Commonweal* countered that whatever the collaborative process may have been, the final product "strikingly parallels the other writings of Novak." As to the group's representativeness:

> Approximately half its members are business executives; others serve on corporate boards. A number are tied to conservative foundations. The group was studded with GOP political figures linked to the Nixon and Reagan administrations (Simon, Haig, Luce, Hiekel, Flanigan, Shakespeare, and Ture); there were no comparable Democrats. Indeed the handful of Democrats included those like Novak and Finn who have supported President Reagan. The group's two union officials resigned.[30]

Commonweal was clearly more pleased by the first draft of *Economic Justice for All: Catholic Social Teaching and the U.S. Economy.* The editors noted the letter's attention to the vast disparities in income and wealth in U.S. society. Such extreme maldistribution, said *Commonweal*, was not necessary for economic growth. "Other capitalist economies outperform ours in many respects, and yet feature far more equitable distribution of income." *Commonweal* quoted the *New York Times*'s remark about the bishops' "clear-eyed view of actual conditions" and welcomed the practical approach of the letter and its challenge to American creativity. What faced the United States, said *Commonweal*, was "not the question of leveling capitalism for some state-directed monolith," but the question as to "whether the creativity we prize in regard to material products can also be applied to social and economic institutions—or whether we have abandoned that creativity somewhere in America's past."[31]

In addition to the editorial, *Commonweal* also contributed to the broad process of dialogue on the economics pastoral by publishing four responses to the first draft of the letter. These include pieces by Paul Steidl-Meier, an advertising executive in Chicago; F. Byron Nahser, a Jesuit theologian in Los Angeles; Rachel A Willis, an administrator of a democratic management project, and Rudy Oswald, the director of the AFL-CIO's department of economic research in Washington, D. C.[32]

At this time, November 1984, *Commonweal* celebrated its sixtieth anniversary. The event was marked with a special issue devoted to faith and economics. The issue was not specifically focused on the pastoral. It did, however, include a helpful selection of excerpts from *Commonweal* on faith and economics through the previous sixty years, from Thomas F. Woodlock's 1925 defense of the principle of the minimum wage to comments from authors such as Hilaire Belloc, John A. Ryan, Dorothy Day, Virgil Michel, Helder Câmara, Charles Owen Rice, and James O'Gara. Among the essays specifically written for this special double issue, perhaps the most notable was an analysis by the late Michael Harrington of the use of statistics in discussing poverty. His analysis of Charles Murray's influential *Losing Ground* was a major contribution.[33]

In March 1985, the editors contributed further suggestions for the revision of the letter. Among them were to speak in a more distinctively American voice, to address issues of power, to communicate to the middle class, and to strengthen the letter's treatment of economic democracy.[34] With an overwhelming vote of 225 to 9, the third draft of the letter was approved by the bishops in November 1986, with *Commonweal* noting that "the revisions of the pastoral have served it well." The most challenging aspect of the document, according to the editors, was its call for the recognition of basic economic rights in addition to the accepted political and civil ones.[35]

Archbishop Rembert Weakland, of Milwaukee, who headed the bishops' committee that developed the letter, had called the articulation and justification of these economic rights a "major thesis" of the document.[36] *Commonweal* pointed out that the letter placed these rights in a communal rather than an individualist framework. Further, the editors supported these rights "not as passive entitlements to material provision but as active empowerments for communal participation."[37] The document had quoted Pope John XXIII, who declared that "all people have a right to life, food, clothing, shelter, rest, medical care, education, and employment."[38] *Commonweal* recognized that securing these rights might require "an arduous effort at building a cultural consensus." Critics, they noted, were quick to attack any claim to such rights, "though their arguments were redolent of objections that have been made to every extension of power and participation, from the right to vote to public schooling."[39]

The discussion of these and other economic questions was, however, clearly not exhausted, and *Commonweal*'s serious and sustained attention to economic justice through six decades—but none more lively than the 1980s—would necessarily continue.[40]

8

From the Council to the Synod

Pope John Paul II's unexpected announcement in January 1985 of a synod to review the changes initiated by Vatican II caught *Commonweal*, and just about everyone else, by surprise. The senior church historian, Monsignor John Tracy Ellis, said simply, "I would dare to say there is not a person in this country who knows what the pope has in mind."[1]

Commonweal viewed the synod with both hope and apprehension. The prospect of the church's leadership gathering from around the world for a full evaluation of the council's aftermath had, on the face of it, much promise, but, they asked rhetorically, did either Pope John Paul's style or the record of past synods suggest a collegial outcome? Further, they stated, Vatican II was "not all of a single piece." There were divergent emphases in the council's documents. Would an unbalanced "reading" of the council emerge from such a gathering? When, at other synods, bishops had tried to engage in the kind of open discussion that characterized Vatican II, their views had "too often been simply passed by in the final documents." Would this synod be different?[2]

But the editors were self-critical, too. Hadn't they, and others, "underestimated the difficulties of the post-conciliar scene"? Wasn't there a reluctance to engage in vigorous criticism when it might have involved "our side," a reluctance "reinforced by natural solidarity whenever critics and dissenters within the church appeared to be the objects of unhearing or authoritarian censure"?[3]

The potential significance of the approaching synod in November 1985 prompted *Commonweal* to plan one of its most successful series of articles. The title for the series was "Charting a Course: From the Council to the Synod," and it was accompanied by a striking logo. The articles focused on questions such as Catholic identity, women and the church, current moral teaching, the life of prayer, and related themes. A number of distinguished thinkers contributed their perspectives.

Authority: The Divided Legacy

The article by the highly respected American Jesuit theologian Avery Dulles was one of the most notable in the series. Dulles dealt with the important question of authority in the church, outlining developments from the opening address at Vatican II by Pope John XXIII to the then-latest action in 1985 by Cardinal Ratzinger. Pope John had said that, in the past, the church had condemned errors with the greatest severity. "Nowadays, however, the spouse of Christ prefers to make use of the medicine of mercy rather than of severity." In the council, the pope declared, "The church desires to show herself to be the loving mother of all, benign, patient, full of mercy and goodness," spreading everywhere "the fullness of Christian charity." This charity could eradicate the seeds of discord. "Often errors vanish as quickly as they arise, like fog before the sun." Under the influence of this papal leadership, stated Dulles, Vatican II took a positive and noncondemning approach. *The Declaration on Religious Freedom* rejected religious coercion on the ground that the act of faith must be essentially free. "Truth," the document stated, "can impose itself on the human mind only in virtue of its own truth, which wins over the mind with both gentleness and power."[4]

In the *Constitution on the Church* the laity were invited to exercise responsible initiatives, and the dignity of all Christians was affirmed since, through baptism, all participate in the priesthood of Christ. These and other assertions of Vatican II, said Dulles, "raised expectations that church authority, after the council, would be more widely distributed among the faithful and would be exercised with greater moderation." In its direct statements on authority, however, the council, Dulles pointed out, "can scarcely be said to have liberalized the official teaching." The council did, indeed, see the bishops as a college succeeding the college of the apostles and thus as having supreme teaching and governing authority in the church. At the same time, the council did not see this as detracting from the supreme authority of the pope. Catholics, according to the council, were obliged to accept in faith what the pope and bishops proclaimed as a matter of faith. When the pope asserted a definite position by his ordinary magisterium without speaking *ex cathedra* (infallibly), the faithful were obliged to assent as a matter of *obsequium religiosum* (religious deference).[5]

The statements on religious authority stood in some tension with the statements emphasizing freedom and tolerance. The council "did not squarely face," said Dulles, the question about the rights and duties of the Catholic who is conscientiously convinced that the official church has erred on a given point. The conflict was evident at the council itself, since many of its theological experts, such as John Courtney Murray, had been  at odds with the Roman magisterium under Pius XII. Indirectly the council had spoken by abstaining from the reaffirmation of recent papal teaching on various subjects—such as the primary end of marriage—and by its reversal of the teaching of previous popes on religious freedom and other matters. Still, the council testimony on authority presented "a divided legacy."

Because its various statements and actions pointed in different directions, the council had not been easy to implement.

Paul VI (1963–1978) "strove loyally to implement it in an even-handed way." John Paul II, since 1978, had "shown himself primarily concerned with reestablishing discipline and overcoming what he describes as the 'disarray and division' left in the wake of the council."

In his discussion of the question of doctrinal control and dissent, Dulles revealed how the Holy Office (originally the Holy Office for the Inquisition) had attracted negative criticism at the council. As Cardinal Frings had said: "Its procedures are out of harmony with modern times, are a source of harm to the faithful, and a scandal to those outside the church." Two days before the end of the council, in December 1965, Paul VI changed the name of the Holy Office to the Congregation for the Doctrine of the Faith (CDF), and he gave it the primarily positive mission of encouraging the development of sound doctrine, saying that "since charity excludes fear, we can now more effectively defend the faith by promoting doctrine."

Under John Paul II, the CDF "intensified its activity against doctrinally suspect authors" and since Joseph Ratzinger had been brought to Rome as its prefect in November 1981, the CDF had "redoubled its concern for orthodoxy." Dulles gave a long list of CDF actions and concluded:

> Our narrative ends, therefore, very much where it began. The CDF under Ratzinger is not unlike the Holy Office under Ottaviani, except that it no longer functions as predictably as the neo-scholastic juridicism of earlier generations enabled it to do. There is little to prevent condemnations from depending on the personal theological view—or even, for that matter, the animosities—of a few highly placed individuals.

Dulles viewed strong structures of authority as an asset to the Catholic church, but he added that "ways must be sought to protect the integrity of the faith without creating even the semblance of unfairness and repression."[6]

The Discipleship of Equals

"Charting a Course: From the Council to the Synod" included an article on women, "The Discipleship of Equals," written by the noted theologian Elisabeth Schussler Fiorenza.[7] She reported in the essay her excitement and the sense of hope that the events of the council stirred within her. The council of bishops took seriously Pope John's vision of a "pastoral" council that would encourage, not condemn; that would "open the windows" so that fresh air—the spirit of life—could blow through the church; that would set free the church's energies for advancing God's reign of truth and justice, love and peace. The twenty years since the council, Fiorenza said, had "proved that these were not just lofty words, but that these were acted upon by countless Catholics, especially by women who have come to experience a new self-identity as women and as church." The twenty years were "a period of struggle," but women, she continued, had "most faithfully sought to put into praxis the spirit of the council for the benefit of the whole church." During those years, women's struggle for the renewal of the church in the spirit of the Gospel had simultaneously strengthened women's struggle in society for justice and truth and vice versa.

In his 1963 encyclical *Pacem in Terris*, Pope John stated that women's struggle for justice and wholeness ought to be recognized by the church. He remarked that "the signs of the times" involved the economic and social advancement of the working classes, the equality of colonial peoples and races, and the participation of women in public life. The council applied this, said Fiorenza, to the participation of  women in the church: "Since in our times women have an ever more active share in the whole life of society, it is very important that they participate more widely in the various fields of the church's apostolate."[8] The council also firmly opposed sexism. On the basis of the fundamental rights of the person, "every type of discrimination, whether social or cultural, whether based on sex, race, color, social condition, language, or religion, is to be overcome and eradicated as contrary to God's intent."[9] After stating that "by divine institution the Holy Church is structured and governed with a wonderful diversity," the *Constitution on the Church* went on to say: "Hence there is in Christ and in the Church no inequality on the basis of race or nationality, social condition or sex."[10]

In the past twenty years, Fiorenza continued, "women in the church had taken these words of the Fathers of this most sacred Council seriously." They had consistently insisted that women be acknowledged "as human and ecclesial subjects rather than objects of power." They had also applied the teachings of the council to the institutional structures of the church and had maintained that human and ecclesial dignity and rights are violated by institutional sexism. The credibility of the church and its proclamation of salvation depended on the rejection of domination and violation of human rights within its own life and structures. Fiorenza quoted the statement of the 1971 synod of bishops on *Justice in the World*, "While the church is bound to give witness to justice, it recognizes that anyone who ventures to speak to others about justice must first be just in their eyes. Hence we must undertake an examination of the modes of acting, of the possessions and lifestyle found within the church itself."[11]

The call to conversion from ecclesiastical patriarchy, however, noted Fiorenza, "had met with increasing rejection by the Vatican," which had appealed to the authority of Christ, the apostles, and tradition in order to legitimate patriarchal church structures that exclude women from sacramental, doctrinal, and governing power on the basis of sex. The struggle for women's ecclesial dignity and rights, however, was "more than a struggle to incorporate a few token women into the lowest ranks of the patriarchy in and through ordination." Instead of the "incorporation of some women into the pyramid of domination," those in this struggle had called "for the conversion of the whole church to the discipleship community of equals which Jesus initiated, the apostolic churches continued, and Vatican II reaffirmed."[12]

Although many church structures were derived from patriarchal Greco-Roman structures of household and state, the church as an institution was not bound to them. Some council texts stressed the hierarchical nature of the church and the ruling power of the clergy, but the council also made clear that the church, in virtue of its mission and nature, was not bound to any "particular form of human culture, nor to any political, economic, or social system."[13]

Was Fiorenza engaging in a selective reading of the conciliar texts? Wouldn't Cardinal Ratzinger present his own selective reading? Fiorenza granted that Ratzinger, in his intrepretation, "might very well consider women's rising consciousness in a patriarchal church structure as one of the errors, abuses, or exaggerations of an indiscriminate opening to the world, since women in traditional theology were identified with the body, the flesh, the world, and even sin and evil." But, she added, the council did not share that particular view of women, but rather called on them "to bring the spirit of this council into institutions, schools, and daily life." She believed that women had faithfully sought to fulfill that commission of Vatican II.[14]

More Voices for the Dialogue

The articles by Dulles and Fiorenza were part of a series of six articles.[15] *Commonweal* completed its discussion of "Charting a Course: From the Council to the Synod" by inviting twenty-one Catholics to share their thoughts on their personal experience and perspective on this pivotal quarter-century of life. These men and women came from diverse occupational and economic backgrounds, were of various age groups, held a wide range of political views, and had quite different personal histories. They all, nonetheless, recognized Catholicism as a major force in their lives. Each was asked:

> How have the promises of Vatican II and the actual changes in the American church since the council affected you? Can you pinpoint developments in your own faith and identity as a Catholic which

resulted from the council and its aftermath? What are the most important shifts, positive or negative, that you have experienced? And what remains the most essential unfinished business still facing the Catholic church today?[16]

The resulting essays were articulate, critical, searchingly honest, and generally reflected an unpretentious but impressive religious authenticity. For author and columnist Garry Wills, the mystery in the church had been dissipated. The result was "more prosaic, but honester . . . the basic thing we owe to God."[17] J. Peter Grace, the chairman and chief executive officer of W. R. Grace and Co., writing as "a practicing Catholic for seventy some years" and as a father of nine and grandfather of fourteen, saw clear gains in liturgical renewal and ecumenism. But he also felt that continuing work had to be done in education in order to pass along the heritage of the church, and family life needed to be encouraged and supported by the church "through realistic, pastorally sound solutions to the many practical problems facing families."[18] Barbara Grizzuti Harrison was raised as a Jehovah's Witness. When she became a writer and attended literary parties she "met only lapsed Catholics, who told boozy lapsed Catholic stories." Later, she walked into St. Patrick's and told the priest on duty that she wanted instruction toward becoming a Catholic (she did eventually convert to Catholicism). She said, "I'd like to have known my church before Vatican II, for better or for worse." She went on to say "others suffered and changed and rejoiced as a result of Vatican II or gave up before Vatican II. . . . And I wonder if I might not have been a better Christian—I'm not a very good one—if I'd had to go through the Before and After process."[19] Joseph Sobran, a senior editor of the *National Review*, felt the post–Vatican II years brought "a huge theological meltdown." The Catholic church in America was becoming too Americanized. "Religion in America, in keeping with the national character, tends to be functional, convenient, utilitarian—a consumer good like microwave ovens and fast food joints, tailored to impatient people who just like to feel good, who don't even comprehend the idea of authority." Sobran said that eventually he saw that the battle within the American church was really revolving around birth control. "Contraceptives are the ultimate consumer goods. They make sex and children matters of consumption."[20]

Mary Durkin was a suburban homemaker and mother of three small children at the beginning of the council. Twenty-five years later she was still a suburban homemaker, and, by that time, a mother of seven young adult children. Inspired by a comment that Hans Küng made in 1964 on the need for lay women theologians, Durkin attended graduate school. By 1974 she had received her doctorate in theology, had become a pastoral theologian with two books on marital intimacy to her name, and, with her brother, Father Andrew Greeley, had co-authored three books: *A Church to Come Home To* (Thomas More, 1982), *How To Save The Church* (Viking, 1984), and *Angry Catholic Women* (Thomas More, 1984). She said she was excited about the contemporary church. "I'm convinced that the Catholic heritage will survive even the most inept statement that might come from the forthcoming synod." The future of the church did not depend on synods, she believed, but rather on reflection on the relationship between the mystery of human experience and the "exciting" God found in the stories, symbols, and practices of a long and rich Catholic tradition. Vatican II had "paved the way to our discovery that religious issues, not institutional and theological issues, must be addressed if the church is to be responsive to the world."[21]

Raymond Flynn, the mayor of Boston, said Vatican II had shown the church's willingness to look outside itself and embrace the world around it. He felt that the pastoral letter on economic justice was in this tradition and showed the church to be "an active force in times of apathy."[22] Author Wilfrid Sheed, *Commonweal's* book editor and drama critic from 1964 to 1966, supported a "predominantly European" view that Vatican II had given ratification to a revolution that had already happened. This had kept "cultural Catholics" hanging around in the shadows near the door. "Without the Council, they would be gone forever," said Sheed. As it was, they "at least are not tempted to leave the church any further than they have."[23]

Several participants mentioned the problems of women in the church. Tom Fox, editor of the *National Catholic Reporter*, said: "My older daughter, eleven, is already asking about her place in the institutional church. The process starts simply enough; she has a brother, twelve. 'Why can Daniel . . . ?,' she asks. My answers are inadequate. Are my children to face unnecessary barriers? And as a result go their own ways?"[24] Sister Camille D'Arienzo, with thirty-four years of service in the Sisters of Mercy, felt that American women represented "a conundrum for the Roman Church." The Vatican was unable to comprehend the pluralism, diversity, or participatory nature of the church in the United States, and targeted women "for the kind of control afforded classes of people in marginalized societies."[25] Nancy Rambusch felt that Americans "suffered neither the historical fatigue nor the cynicism of Europeans" and expected that our postconciliar institutions would reflect a change and renewal "that would encompass women as well as men." Rambusch, a mother and early childhood educator, wondered how the church that continued to exclude women from its ruling councils ever expected to reflect their "presence" in shaping its present and future agendas.[26]

An overall sense of hope and religious meaning permeated the responses. Palma E. Formica, a medical doctor from New Jersey, wrote that, for her, Vatican II was the affirmation of what she believed:

> We are each called to love and serve God with talents generously bestowed. "Brotherhood" with Christ includes even non-Catholics and non-believers. We can accept ourselves and our failures, because we are loved and forgiven by a gracious God who loves us unceasingly. We are the church: a royal priesthood but still a pilgrim people. The Good News is critically relevant to our lives today.

Concerning the institutional church, Formica remarked that Pope John XXIII was a reminder to her that change had happened and that "hope and confidence in a sinful, 'holy church' is not incongruous."[27]

Jean Vanier, founder of *l'Arche*, a community for mentally handicapped youths and adults in France, wrote of his encounter with a conservative Catholic who, in his fearful assessment in the years following Vatican II, said: "They have thrown out the baby with the bath water!" Vanier's rejoinder: "No, the baby is still there and the bath water is still dirty!"[28]

Tom Fox wrote of his "many debts to our church's formal structures."

> They helped form the piety and faith of my Polish mother, the wisdom of my father, a scientist, who viewed his profession as an act of love, the mapping out of God's divine mystery. They molded my formal Catholic education during which I was passed from prayerful, selfless nuns to eager and educated Jesuits, and through a host of other religious who ushered me along the way. And how could I have met my wife, a Catholic convert in a faraway land, were it not for this Eucharistic network we call church? At the center are values of love and reconciliation, the search for justice and peace, notions of human family and personal dignity, the good news of God's unending concern. It is all this I wish to pass to our children, as it has been passed to me through the church, old and new.[29]

Peter Quinn attended Manhattan College—and eventually taught there—served as a VISTA volunteer in Kansas City, taught in a Catholic high school, received a graduate degree in Irish history from Fordham, became a speech writer for Hugh Carey and Mario Cuomo, and worked as an assistant to the president of Time, Inc. He described his own religious journey "back to the Catholic tradition I had been nurtured in . . . the sense of human frailty and imperfectibility, the rituals of penance and communion, the shared struggle across the centuries of frail, flawed, sinful human beings to touch the mystery of God's love, to embody it, to live it, to be saved by it." This postconciliar church was more disorderly, but it was a church "infinitely more alive and spirited, a company of pilgrims who are Catholic by choice."

> I have no nostalgia for the old order, the safe but stultifying fortress I knew as a child. This pilgrim church, trying to reconcile change and tradition, timeless truth and the vagaries of human metaphor, is my home. It is a ramshackle place where the roof may occasionally leak, and the walls may be cracked, and the people upstairs are sometimes overbearing, but it is home nonetheless, the context of my life.[30]

"Charting a Course: From the Council to the Synod" received a good deal of praise, but Clare Huchet-Bishop, a well-known author of children's books, wrote from Paris of her distress that none of the participants had mentioned Vatican II's highly significant *Declaration on the Jews*.[31] Similarly, the distinguished Protestant theologian Harvey Cox questioned why no non-Catholics had been asked for their views on the subject. "When John XXIII opened the window, we *all* benefited from the fresh air that swept in. If it is closed we will all begin to suffocate again."[32]

"No Victors and No Vanquished" ran the headline in the *New York Times* over its story on the synod itself. "Who won the synod?," Cardinal Law of Boston was quoted as saying. "I think the church won the synod." In Peter Steinfels's assessment: "Perhaps there were no victors or vanquished, but I am not sure the church won either." Steinfels did not feel that the synod was a setback and believed that some degree of respect had been shown for the national episcopal conferences and some "serious gestures of renewed concern for ecumenism" had been made. On the other hand, he surmised that the synod's clear expression of concern for collegiality would probably not affect Rome's apparent determination to "use its powers of appointment, its censure of theologians, its pressures on religious orders as it sees fit and quite regardless of the advice of America's bishops, to say nothing of any consideration for the views of the rest of us."[33]

Before the synod, the Irish-born theologian Father Paul Surlis had written in *Commonweal* that it was the clear intention of Vatican II to recommend the institution of a synod in order to provide a system of checks-and-balances against curial bureaucracy. This curial bureaucracy should be the civil service of the papacy and the bishops. In practice, however, said Surlis, the curia functioned "as a bureaucracy *over* the college of bishops."[34]

Elisabeth Schussler Fiorenza saw the synod in a more negative light than Peter Steinfels had. The synod had been "a visual demonstration of the patriarchal church," she wrote. This completely male gathering had issued a formidable list of the ills of the world in its "message to the People of God," but patriarchal sexism was never mentioned. She found some hope in one of the themes proposed by the synod: the church as *koinonia*/communion—shared partnership and commitment—which, she said, was "pregnant with possibilities for Catholic theology and ecclesiology in the post-synodal period." Among her specific suggestions: as long as the college of bishops is restricted to men, the college of cardinals should be restricted to women. "Since the collegium of cardinals does not go back to Jesus nor stand in apostolic succession nor require ordination, no presumed theological obstacle would stand in the way of such a suggestion," she concluded.[35]

Eugene McCarthy, the former senator from Minnesota who ran as an independent candidate for president in 1968, didn't think the synod could turn back much of what had happened nor could it "reverse or turn aside some of the strong currents now running in the church, such as the changing concept of the priesthood, including the issue of the ordination of women."[36] Tom Fox had seen the calling of this extraordinary synod as "an opportunity to solidify a pastoral vision of church, and a notion of faith, not simply as knowledge, but as an entire way of life." And what if the opportunity was lost or misused? "We will continue on the journey. There's no going back. Simple as that."[37]

9

Commonweal in the Late Eighties

In May of 1986, faced with a steep increase in rent, *Commonweal* made a decision to depart the midtown Manhattan office it had occupied for a quarter century. Its new location, 15 Dutch Street, on a block-long unfashionable street not far from Wall Street, brought savings of $95,000 that would accrue over a five-year period. But the new space required extensive renovation and immediate cash that simply wasn't available. Operating revenues for 1985 had fallen $80,000 short of expenses. Although the Commonweal Associates had grown in number from 202 in 1961 to 545 in 1986, and had contributed $52,500 toward offsetting costs,[1] publisher Ed Skillin felt that they couldn't afford to move. Editor Peter Steinfels, however, felt that they couldn't afford not to move. There was little time to choose and no time at all to make an appeal to readers for contributions because a decision had to be made immediately. Steinfels pushed for making the move on the gamble that their faithful readers (*Commonweal* has a remarkably high 80 percent renewal rate) would see them through. Skillin, at eighty-two and with fifty-three years of work invested in *Commonweal*, agreed to take the risk.[2]

Steinfels's letter of appeal described the background of the situation and affirmed the faith of *Commonweal* in its mission and in its readers. While there was a rising tide of interest in the questions and issues that had always been *Commonweal's* special focus, there was little doubt that much of what the magazine stood for was "under particularly sharp challenge."

> The so-called new conservatism takes many forms, from the sophisticated to the savage, from the philosophical to the fanatic. Often enough, however, its practical prescription for every ill boils down to the same thing: "get tough." Getting tough means the resort to arms in international affairs, the *ipse dixit* [an assertion made on authority but not proven] of authority in moral and philosophical questions, the sink-or-swim attitude toward those at the bottom of the economic order. One need not argue that getting tough is never called for; but it is certainly a strategy more congenial to the powerful than the powerless, the vulnerable or the poor. And the powerful are duly using their considerable resources to fund dozens of right-of-center think tanks, policy journals, professorships, campus publications, and newsletters.

Steinfels said he didn't begrudge these forces their exceptional capacity to propagate their views, but he was concerned that *Commonweal's* views continue to be heard. He was especially concerned that *Commonweal* not become, as too many journals and groups had, the mirror image of what they were *against*. "A journal which maintains its convictions while respecting complexity and ambiguity has a special role to play amidst today's polarizations," he wrote. Expressing faith in *Commonweal* readers, he said the appeal "constitutes a real gamble on our part," but "it's not really a leap in the dark."[3]

By November 1986, Steinfels was able to report that the faith in *Commonweal's* readership had been "well placed." The renovations, the move itself, and other costs, such as printing stationery, had been more than anticipated, but gifts and pledges amounting to $60,000 had *Commonweal* "steaming ahead" and served to remind the staff that *Commonweal's* readers were "its greatest strength." The staff was overwhelmed by the notes accompanying the donations, which expressed great gratitude for the magazine's service over the years. Mrs. Joseph A. Lambert said she had been at the meeting in 1924 when Michael Williams introduced *Commonweal,* and she had been "a fan ever since." Monsignor John J. O'Hara of St. Leo's parish in Hot Springs, California, said: "Things are bleak at present in old mother church. We need your independent and sane voice—hang in there!" Milton Raisbeck, M.D., said: "The independent spirit of *Commonweal* is a constant solace, a stimulus and an encouragement that both maintains and strengthens my faith in human nature. More power to you."[4] These and hundreds of other such notes were circulated and read by every staff member and made a special impact.

In addition to the new home—modest but modern and efficient—*Commonweal* had a new look in 1987. The new page format and design was created by Emil Antonucci, a teacher at the Parsons School of Design who had worked on the previous logo change in 1965. The editors explained that, of necessity, *Commonweal* was printed on inexpensive paper stock, which could easily give the magazine a "gray" look. The new design employed striking rules and heavy initials to counter this tendency and give some bold contrast to the pages. The typeface, Gill Ultra, was designed by Eric Gill (1882–1940), the English sculptor, wood engraver, typographer, and artisan-philosopher, some of whose writings had appeared in *Commonweal.*[5]

In 1989, the most dramatic change in appearance in *Commonweal's* history occurred when the magazine turned from "gray" to white. The cause was a new grade of paper—groundwood matte—a white stock that offered greater contrast to the typeface and led to much easier reading. This was achieved with no increase of costs.[6] By chance, Emil Antonucci's article "Our Task Is to Create Worlds: An Artist and the Experience of God" in the *Commonweal* series "The Laity and the Life of Faith" appeared in the first issue on the new paper.[7] The series was not a collection of the reflections of professional theologians who happened to be lay persons, but a collection of reflections that expressed a distinctive and quite authentic lay theology.

Legal ownership of *Commonweal* changed in 1982. The existing arrangement had begun in 1938 when, in the midst of a financial and personnel crisis, legal ownership of the magazine had been transferred from the Calvert Publishing Corporation to the Commonweal Publishing Company, Inc. Philip Burnham, then twenty-seven, and Edward Skillin, then thirty-three, two junior *Commonweal* editors who had been with the magazine since 1933, purchased the magazine for $9,000. That amount went toward settling debts with *Commonweal*'s paper supplier, printer, and landlord.[8] In establishing the Commonweal Publishing Company, however, young Burnham and Skillin did not incorporate on a nonprofit basis though that was in fact the reality of the enterprise. Within a decade, Burnham had withdrawn from any active association with *Commonweal*, and in the late 1950s he sold his stock in the magazine to Skillin, making Skillin, in effect, the sole owner. Two major reasons were behind the shift of ownership to the nonprofit Commonweal Foundation in 1982. First, Skillin, at seventy-seven, wanted to ensure that *Commonweal* would have the legal basis on which to continue its work after his death, and second, there were the advantages of nonprofit status in terms of funding. The board of directors of the new Commonweal Foundation consisted of Edward S. Skillin as president, James O'Gara as vice president, Peter Steinfels as secretary-treasurer, with Paul V. Farrell and Daniel M. Murtaugh as directors. Farrell was a long-time *Commonweal* supporter, who had married Theodora Cogley, widow of the late John Cogley. Murtaugh served as an assistant editor at the magazine from 1979 to 1980 and had since been an employee of W. R. Grace & Co.

In November 1987 a special meeting of the board was convened for a very important reason. Peter Steinfels had decided to accept a new position as the senior religion correspondent for the *New York Times*, and *Commonweal* would need a new editor. Steinfels had first joined *Commonweal* in 1964 and remained on the staff through 1971. His column continued throughout the 1970s. He rejoined the staff in 1978 as executive editor and became editor in 1984 upon the retirement of

James O'Gara. Steinfels had received overtures from the *New York Times* before. Now, however, people at the top of the *Times*'s organization were seeking his services with an offer that would more than double his salary. Steinfels notes that salary was not a decisive consideration, however. This seems true or he likely would have more actively pursued the earlier overtures from the *Times*. But in addition to the solid proposition from the *Times,* there was a sense that he had made his impact on *Commonweal,* maybe not in all particulars but substantially nonetheless. He had led the move to Dutch Street, which was very successful; he had played an important role in securing legal help and facilitating the establishment of the Commonweal Foundation; and, although he had been editor for less than four years, he had played a very significant leadership role in the conduct of the magazine in the full decade after his return as executive editor. In addition, he was simply tired. The multiple and open-ended demands of editing, writing editorials, promoting, fundraising, and cover design, while exhilarating, were also exhausting. The *Times* presented a fresh challenge and a wider audience, but more limited responsibilities. The fact that John Cogley had been the first occupant of the post he was assuming at the *Times* certainly crossed his mind, but it was not a pivotal consideration.

To find a new editor for *Commonweal,* Steinfels drafted a proposal for a national search process. As the special meeting of the Board of Directors of the Commonweal Foundation approached, he also, in conversation with his wife, Margaret (Peggy) O'Brien Steinfels, asked if she were considering applying for the position. She replied that she was giving it thought but was uncertain whether she would apply. The board considered a wide list of possible candidates, but Jim O'Gara and the other members felt that Peggy Steinfels was, in fact, their top potential candidate. Further, if she were so obviously the candidate they would choose, didn't it make sense to pursue her directly? O'Gara, a former editor and now a director, was delegated to ask her if she would be willing to talk about the position. Knowing that Peter had proposed a complicated search process to the board, Peggy Steinfels was taken aback when O'Gara called her and shared the board's thinking. She recalls:

I wanted to say, "Yes, Yes!" On the other hand, I wanted to say, and did, "Are you sure you've thought carefully about this? Do you realize it's a bit uncomfortable for me and the magazine?" He understood me, I think, but he still wanted me to come talk to the Board. And I did, and it was a wonderful, down-to-earth interview. . . . In the end, they offered me the job and I said what I'd always wanted to say.

The report of the board states:

Charged with the duty of selecting a replacement as Editor, the Board of Directors of the Commonweal Foundation began its search without prior commitments. At the first special meeting of the Board, a broad list of potential candidates was surveyed. At that time the immediate and unanimous feeling of the Board members, minus Mr. Steinfels' participation, was that an outstanding candidate for the position was at hand. She had a demonstrated record in directing journals of this sort, including experience on the business as well as editorial side of magazine publishing. She had written widely on religious, ethical and social issues. She had established an independent voice that reflected the concerns for which *Commonweal* has long been noted. That candidate was Margaret O'Brien Steinfels. . . . In a subsequent meeting, with Mr. Steinfels continuing to absent himself from the discussion, the Board interviewed the candidate at length, carefully reviewed her qualifications, and confirmed its earlier impression.[9]

The board voted unanimously to select Margaret O'Brien Steinfels as the new editor of *Commonweal*. Her duties began with the first issue of 1988.

Margaret Steinfels was an honors graduate of Loyola University in Chicago. She later took courses at Columbia University and the Sorbonne and earned an M.A. in history at New York University. She had written *Who's Minding the*

Children?, a well-received history and political analysis of child care in America and had contributed chapters to other books as well as to publications such as the *National Catholic Reporter, New Catholic World,* the *New York Times,* the *Los Angeles Times, Psychology Today, Jubilee,* and *Commonweal.* In the 1970s she was editor of the *Hastings Center Report,* the leading journal in the field of bioethics. She served as social science editor at Basic Books. At *Christianity and Crisis,* a distinguished ecumenical biweekly founded by Reinhold Niebuhr, she began her employ as business manager and adanced to executive editor and columnist. In 1985, she had become director of publications for the National Pastoral Life Center and founding editor of *Church,* a quarterly published by the center. The report of the Commonweal Foundation board stated that it recognized that even in an age that discusses "which Dole should run for president," it was unusual for an outgoing editor to be replaced by a spouse, but it was their conviction that "the leading candidate should not be excluded for this reason."[10]

As far back as 1945, founding editor Michael Williams stated that the original owners, the Calvert Associates, included a number of women as well as men, "something which shouldn't be forgotten in our masculine-muddled America."[11] Through the years, however, only a small number of women have served on the *Commonweal* editorial staff. Helen Walker left the *New Republic* to become an assistant editor on the original staff. When she married three years later, she left *Commonweal.* Later, she resumed her career, becoming a journalism professor and authoring two books. Mary Kolars replaced Helen Walker as assistant editor in 1927 and stayed until 1938 when she became an editor at St. Anthony's Press. There was then an absence of women on *Commonweal's* small staff until Anne Fremantle joined as associate editor in 1947. She was already, at that time, the most frequent contributor of articles and reviews to the magazine. The author and editor of many books, she shifted to a part-time contributing editor status in 1952 and continued in that post until 1958. Oona Sullivan, who had been managing editor of *Jubilee,* joined *Commonweal* as an associate editor in 1967, serving only in an interim capacity while Peter Steinfels spent a year in Paris. When Raymond A. Schroth, S. J., became an assistant editor in 1972, the debate in the hiring process was not about having yet another male editor, but about whether the essentially lay character of *Commonweal* would be changed by having a Jesuit priest as an editor. (Jim O'Gara recalls that issue being settled by a group decision that *Commonweal* "shouldn't make a fetish out of the laity thing.")[12] Of the thirty-nine persons who served on the editorial staff of *Commonweal* through its first fifty years, only four were women.

Anne Robertson, who joined *Commonweal* as an editorial assistant in 1965, and then became production editor in 1984, observed the changing presence and role of women at the magazine, especially after 1979. She herself was part of that process. John Fandel concluded sixteen distinguished years as poetry editor in 1979 (*Commonweal* publishes about fifty poems a year) and was succeeded by Rosemary Deen and Marie Ponsot. Deen and Ponsot carried on the prize-winning tradition that, as George Shuster once noted, has made many friends for the magazine, and creatively served its readers.[13] The presence of Abigail McCarthy's regular column, which has been continuous since the mid-1970s, was another example of the trend toward hiring more female staff members.[14] There was also growth in the number of women seeking editorial positions at *Commonweal*. Its part-time editorial opening in 1979 drew applications from twenty-three men and six women. The full-time position available in 1984 drew thirty-nine men and thirty-one women.[15] It was at that time that Karen Sue Smith and Patrick Jordan became assistant editors. When Margaret O'Brien Steinfels became editor, the only full-time male editor on staff was Patrick Jordan. David Toolan was an associate editor along with Smith and Jordan, but Toolan's part-time role made him present in the *Commonweal* office only two days a week. Although Edward Skillin was a regular presence in the office, he largely confined himself to his duties as publisher and was not directly involved in editorial matters. Those present every day were Margaret Steinfels, associate editors Karen Sue Smith and Patrick Jordan, and production editor Anne Robertson. Rosemary Deen, as poetry editor, was an occasional presence as was Tom O'Brien,

Commonweal's movie critic. In 1989, Robert G. Hoyt, who was the founding editor of the *National Catholic Reporter* and later an editor at *Christianity and Crisis,* joined *Commonweal* as senior writer. Later that year, Anne Robertson died at age fifty-seven from cancer. She had served the magazine for thirty years. Despite her modest title, she may well be the woman who influenced *Commonweal* more than any other in its first sixty-five years. As John Deedy said in his eulogy, Anne Robertson "was a large part of *Commonweal*'s editorial and ideological conscience."[16]

The roll of important women who helped *Commonweal,* however, would not be complete without the mention of Kathleen Casey Craig, who served for many years as president of the Commonweal Associates. As Ed Skillin commented in 1989, when she died, "In the 1940s when the magazine found itself on the sheer margin of survival, month after month 'Honey' Craig purchased preferred shares of stock in the struggling Commonweal Publishing Company." She served as a director of the company for a number of years and made substantial contributions to the associates.[17] The current president of the Commonweal Associates is another woman, Sidney Callahan.

10

New Leadership for a Continuing Tradition

Commonweal's commitment to the commonweal—the common or shared well-being of all— and its self identification as "a review of public affairs, religion, literature and the arts" continued when Margaret O'Brien Steinfels became its first female editor in its sixty-third year of existence. Peggy Steinfels and her associate editors, David Toolan, Karen Sue Smith, and Patrick Jordan took turns contributing editorials that followed the usual wide range of *Commonweal* interests. Editorials in the first issue under the new editorship challenged the tailoring of the definition of death to the requirements of obtaining organ transplants; commended "The Many Faces of AIDS: A Gospel Response," the document issued by the administrative board of the U. S. Catholic Conference; and discussed the problem of hunger in America, citing reports of the U. S. Conference of Mayors and the Harvard Physician Task Force on Hunger in the U. S., which stated that twenty million Americans go hungry part of each month.[1] Editorials in the subsequent issue spoke of racism as "a more complicated and elusive foe than Americans imagined twenty years ago"; noted the problems and some hopeful possibilities in the apparent impasse between Israelis and Palestinians; and questioned the approach of the *National Catholic Reporter*'s special issue on peacemaking that had featured contributions by several distinguished Catholic pacifists while giving no space to peacemakers who worked within the just war tradition.[2] A brief editorial in the same issue, entitled "A Resourceful 17 Years," noted that *Commonweal*'s presence in "new quarters on an obscure alley in Lower Manhattan after a quarter century on high rent Madison Avenue" was attributable to Peter Steinfels. The attractive and well-planned offices in a lower-rent area were "tangible evidence of all that Peter put into *Commonweal* in some seventeen productive years." But this visible accomplishment "pales when measured against what he has done in the magazine itself over the years." Steinfels was praised as "a versatile person who has been generously applying his manifold talents to giving effective Christian witness in a troubled time."[3]

Partners in the Mystery of Redemption

The first draft of a pastoral response by U.S. Catholic bishops to women's concerns was released in April 1988. The purpose of *Partners in the Mystery of Redemption* was "to report the results of extensive consultations with women, to reflect on this input in the light of our Christian heritage and to offer responses and recommendations, not as final conclusions but as contributions to ongoing dialogue and appropriate action in homes, schools, parishes and dioceses."[4]

Commonweal said that the pastoral letter showed that the bishops had "come a long way," though they still had "a long way to go." The editors praised the genuine listening that had taken place during the preparation of the draft. "The testimony of tens of thousands of women before diocesan commissions and national organizations, and in hearings organized by the drafting committee, has been heard and the bishops have taken it to heart." The document included many quotes from the hearings—words of sorrow, pain, outrage, and disagreement as well as of appreciation and praise, words and experiences "that the six member drafting committee could not appropriately speak itself." In the bishops' own responses were "echoes of the painful examination of conscience that they clearly have had to undertake on hearing these critical words." In some cases, predictable restatements of church teaching—for example, the prohibition against women's ordination—were "couched with explicit and courteous recognition of widespread questioning by theologians and others." In other cases more direct changes were proposed by the bishops, with the opening of the diaconate and minor orders to women, noted *Commonweal*, "virtually endorsed." The document had given a clear-cut declaration that sexism is a moral and social evil and had enumerated its evils in both blatant and subtle forms: rape, pornography, exploitation, abuse, job and wage discrimination, contempt, and condescending words and behavior. It held that attitudes tending toward sexism or an incapacity to deal with women as equals should be judged as "negative indications for fitness for ordination," and it called all men to examine patterns and attitudes that regard women as inferior.

In addition to finding strengths in the draft, the editors also found weaknesses. They felt the pastoral was "not a work of critical analysis." The committee had not conducted a public inquiry or written a draft "at the same level of theoretical sophistication as the pastorals on the economy and on war and peace." The emphasis on experiences and feelings overshadowed fact and analysis. The overall framework, while it was a great strength in airing criticisms and grievances, became a barrier to considering the concerns of women because of their accomplishments, both from a personal as well as a career perspective. *Commonweal* further stated that the carefully crafted words on women's ordination struck them "as an equivocation and evasion of the church's own sin of sexism," while the continued absolute opposition to contraception in marriage crippled the church's credibility. Overall, however, the letter was "a cause for hope and a starting point for a new conversation."[5] Both the editorial and Abigail McCarthy's subsequent column noted that only a decade or two ago such a pastoral letter could not have been written.[6]

In June 1988, *Commonweal* published six responses to the draft of the pastoral, including both Catholic and Protestant respondents. Author Jane Redmont cheered what was "above all a testimony to a conversion process" and wondered how far the bishops would have the courage to carry their process and reflections. She groaned, however, at what she felt was the bishops' evasion of a critical reevaluation of the absolute opposition to the use of contraception in marriage. Theologian Anne Patrick noted that whereas specialists in ethics were notably involved in drafting the other two pastorals there was no evidence of such direct impact on this pastoral. "It may be, of course, that the limits set by Rome have ruled out from the start the most logical source of theologically trained analysis, for few if any Catholic women moral theologians are persuaded that official teachings on contraception and women's ordination can be justified in our day." All six women respondents found some measure of hope in the document while making various criticisms and suggestions.[7] Correspondent Ed Marciniak commended the responses but asked why women only? "Sexism and feminism, in their own way, are issues which command a response from men. Women and men have to dialogue unless the pastoral is to be viewed only as a letter of the bishops to women alone."[8]

Anniversary Waltz

The twentieth anniversary of *Humanae Vitae*, the 1968 papal encyclical on contraception, prompted a long and thoughtful editorial in *Commonweal*. In some quarters, the anniversary was being celebrated, the editors noted, as the great dividing line between those who are faithful to the church and those who are not. Faithfulness to the church, "to the Gospel proclaimed and witnessed by Jesus' disciples, and guided and enlivened by the Spirit," is essential, but "faithfulness is not blind assent to assertions of authority."

> Who was more faithful a century ago? Those who insisted upon the "doctrine" that the temporal power of the pope and his sovereignty over the papal states was required to assure his independence—or those who questioned it? "Temporal power" was a teaching repeated no less incessantly

and vehemently—but with a good deal more bloodletting—than the ban on artificial contraception today. It, too, was invested with papal authority and became a standard of loyalty for advancement to important positions of church leadership. And it was wrong.

In 1968, a determination to be faithful to the church led many Catholics to conclude that *Humanae Vitae* was "one of those tragic errors into which the church of Christ has fallen over the centuries, sometimes with the best of intentions but always with long-run damage to its mission."[9]

In a careful rereading of the encyclical twenty years later, the editors found that "for all of the pope's insistence on natural law and the constant teaching of the church, he seems more concerned, at points, with what he saw as the dire consequences of contraception—marital infidelity, a lowering of moral standards, and the lack of incentive for the young to observe the moral law (read: fear of pregnancy)." Paul VI, they felt, was right to worry, and "the terrible human cost of our culture's disarray in sexual matters" was "Exhibit A" for those who currently defended the encyclical, but these defenders needed to be reminded of the logical fallacy of *post hoc, ergo propter hoc* (after this, therefore because of this). Their argument was even more fundamentally flawed since the sexual revolution was already well under way when *Humanae Vitae* appeared. For all of his justifiable concern, Paul VI's conclusions had "hobbled the church for the cultural struggle at hand." Yes, the editors admitted, responsible human sexuality meant drawing lines, but "the sorry outcome, as we now see, was that he drew one of them in the wrong place" and rather than enhancing the church's teaching on sexuality the encyclical "unwittingly undermined it." In the intervening years, clergy and religious and lay teachers, "caught between bishops obedient to the pope and an incredulous laity, became circumspect or fell silent on the subject of sexual morality in pulpits and classrooms." The failure to develop a fuller understanding of marriage and sexual morality had been "especially detrimental to young Catholics," many of whom had followed the culture's lead and had "adopted a contraceptive mentality and the casual sexual relations that go with it." A perplexed world was genuinely searching for moral yardsticks, but the editors maintained that the church's loss of credibility had injured its effort to speak soundly to a potentially receptive public. Perhaps this was clearest in the abortion debate, where "so many have succumbed to the notion that abortion is the subset of the contraception debate and judge the church's teaching equally vulnerable." The editors recalled that, in 1968, *Commonweal* had predicted that the encyclical would "fail the test of history." In 1988, they said that two decades did not make history, but "so far it seems that the encyclical has failed the church."[10]

Meanwhile, more than one hundred people, including several bishops, were attending "Trust the Truth," a conference held in Princeton, New Jersey, celebrating the encyclical's anniversary. It was sponsored by Opus Dei's Roman Academic Center Foundation and the Catholic chaplaincy at Princeton University. There, Canadian Cardinal Edward Gagnon, president of the Pontifical Council for the Family, told participants that *Humanae Vitae* had not been adequately announced and proclaimed and so, for example, in his country, Canada had "changed from a country in which the family was the bulwark of morality to one of the parts of the world with the lowest birthrate." Gagnon said he believed Paul VI received "special help from God" in the proclamation of *Humanae Vitae*. When Gagnon heard rumors that the pope might reverse the teaching of the church, he went to him and asked, "Is it true? We've been fighting like hell, and it's not easy." The pope replied, "Don't be afraid. Twenty years from now everybody will see that I was right about that doctrine."[11]

Published reaction to *Commonweal*'s editorial was mixed. John Cort, a former member of the editorial staff at *Commonweal* in the 1940s and 1950s, wrote to say he had changed his mind from dissent to support of the papal view, after observing the effects of twenty years of the contraceptive mentality. He said also that overpopulation in the world was a myth.[12] *Commonweal* letter writer Frank Arricale, on the other hand, said that Paul VI's tragic mistake, while it brought "enormous anguish of both those who remained on the Bark of Peter and those who jumped ship," did have one beneficial consequence: "A papal fundamentalism, especially on the part of American Catholics, has begun to fade. Rome cannot be viewed as an ecclesiastical automat into which problems are put and answers dished out." Arricale said "this simplistic ecclesiastical fundamentalism" was "as harmful to faith as scriptural fundamentalism."[13]

The editors responded to Cort's assertion by pointing out that in developing countries, unchecked population growth was "one factor among many in the continuing struggle for development." They answered Arricale's letter by reminding readers that *Humanae Vitae* had indeed helped some Catholics rise above "our own church's special form of fundamentalism," but that they only wished this maturity had been acquired in a less costly way, "both for individuals whose faith did not come unscathed through this crisis and for a culture left without persuasive guidance about sex."[14]

In November 1988, another conference was held, "*Humanae Vitae*: 20 Years After," this time at the Lateran University in Rome. The sponsor was again Opus Dei's Roman Academic Center Foundation, teamed up with the John Paul II Institute at the Lateran. The meeting was financed by the Knights of Columbus and arranged by Monsignor Carlo Caffarra, president of the Lateran University and consultant to the Congregation for the Doctrine of the Faith and to the Pontifical Council on the Family. The purpose of this meeting, like the earlier one at Princeton, was not to have a serious exchange of diverse viewpoints but rather to have, what Father Bernard Haring has called, a singing of "the intransigents' hymn of victory." Speaking at the meeting, Pope John Paul II proclaimed that the teaching against contraception was not a doctrine created by human beings, but that it was "written by the creative hand of God in the nature of the human person." Monsignor Caffarra compared contraception to committing "homicide in the heart."[15]

Such rhetoric was one of the reasons for the issuance of the Cologne Declaration by 163 distinguished Catholic theologians from Germany, Austria, the Netherlands, and Switzerland. In 1989, it was translated and published in *Commonweal*.[16] The declaration criticized the attempt to connect the teaching on birth control with the most fundamental truths of the faith and recalled the statement made at Vatican II that held that "in comparing doctrines with one another it should not be forgotten that there is an order of precedence or 'hierarchy' of truths within Catholic doctrine, according to the different ways they are connected with the foundation of Christian faith."[17] The theologians pointed out that conscience "is not an executive assistant to the papal teaching office" and that many in the church were convinced that the norms for birth control in *Humanae Vitae* represented a moral position that did not replace the responsibility of the faithful to their own conscience. They said they regretted "the intense fixation of the papal teaching office on this single problem area."[18] *Commonweal* also reprinted the essay of Bernard Haring from the Italian Catholic magazine *Il Regno*. Haring, a member of the Papal Birth Control Commission, which in 1966 had voted overwhelmingly to accept the responsible use of contraception in marriage, spoke against the inflexible position the Vatican was taking on artificial contraception and against the anonymous denunciations of theologians and other inquisitorial methods. Haring said that "whatever one's opinion on the matter, the problem of prohibiting artificial means of contraception does not occupy a preeminent position in the 'hierarchy of truths.' " But some people—Monsignor Caffarra, for example—had raised the issue to such a level of importance that conflict was unavoidable, and John Paul II had given this problem a clear priority. Haring called for a new worldwide consultation on the question of birth control. "I hope our beloved pontiff understands that we are dealing with a conflict of epic proportions, no less than the one at Antioch between Peter and Paul. The debate must be conducted openly on the basis of dialogue without violence and with mutual love."[19]

The John Courtney Murray Forum Lecture

Margaret O'Brien Steinfels delivered the 1989 John Courtney Murray Forum Lecture at Fordham University on May 18, 1989. The lecture is named for the distinguished Jesuit theologian who is generally considered the architect of Vatican II's

Declaration on Religious Freedom. Her address was printed in
America and was sent with a cover letter by *Commonweal*
publisher Edward Skillin to the *Commonweal* Associates. He
noted that her lecture, "The Church and Its Public Life," was
the product of long reflection and much revision. As such, it
was very much her own. Skillin added, however, that in his
view "it also encapsulates the *Commonweal* tradition of independent, balanced, yet incisive analysis of the American
Catholic church in its public life."[20]

Steinfels argued that the present moment was one in which
the entire direction of the past quarter century seemed to be
at stake. She said that, as one intramural Catholic crisis succeeded another, her particular concern was not with any one
or several of these attention-grabbing events but with "a quiet,
continuing underground crisis, not a heart attack but a kind of
seeping hemorrhage; not a crisis of heresy or free speech but
nonetheless a crisis of truth." It was a crisis "of plausibility, of
credibility, and—speaking as an editor and a writer—a crisis
of language." She illustrated the crisis with three issues: gender, authority, and the relationship of church and world.[21]

Recent official Catholic discussions of gender, she said, had
come to pivot on two terms: *radical feminism* and *complementarity.* "Unfortunately, the current use of 'radical feminism' closes rather than opens discussion, uses a label to
convict without either identifying the accused or arguing the
case." She noted that a recent meeting in Rome had frequently
mentioned radical feminism as a villain, but at a press briefing
after the meeting three prelates offered three definitions, none
attached to specific names, specific writings, or specific claims
of specific feminists. It was a situation in which one saw
"words slipping off the realities." The term *radical feminism*
could mean simply "whatever is more impatient, or more
aggrieved, or more egalitarian than an archbishop."

She then discussed the term *complementarity.* It was indeed
a fact, she said, that there were physiological and psychological differences between men and women, but what exactly
should we make of those differences? This was a subject of
much debate. If women were likely to have tender hearts, as
one curial official had recently warned, did that mean they
could not serve on marriage tribunals, or, on the contrary, did

it mean that no marriage tribunal should be without them? The term *complementarity* came "burdened with a history and a load of assumptions about the link between natural characteristics and social roles increasingly attenuated in the everyday lives of many women and men." Such language seemed to be ultimately calculated "not to name a relevant reality, but to evade real equality in the church."

Concerning authority, Steinfels said that confidence in both structures and spirit was "oozing" away. "Synods of bishops, international commissions, an internationalized and superficially reformed Curia—the gaps open between words and deeds." The very word *collegiality*, once so exciting, was "losing substance." There were two well-worn adages that Steinfels said could be used to conjure away the plausibility crisis in the area of governance and authority:

> One favored by church officials is "The church is not a democracy," usually uttered with a complacent finality. Its populist opposite, usually uttered with proprietary arrogance, is: "We are the church." Both are only partial truths.

To be sure, the church was not a democracy in the sense that no political arrangement could be equated with the body of Christ, but insofar as democracy was the contemporary form through which people affirmed their loyalties, checked abuses of power, directed their reflection, participated as equals, and, in general, protected their dignity, Steinfels contended, there was no reason why the church should not "willingly rather than grudgingly put on democracy." She said that the claim, "We are the church," advanced literally and possessively, could be seen not as democratic at all, but as a sort of coup d'état of the contemporary. "We alone are not the church. Thank God. Perhaps from St. Peter's to *Commonweal*, that should be a daily prayer."

Steinfels's third issue was the relationship of church and world. It was thought, she stated, that Vatican II had achieved a decisive shift in the church's understanding of its stance toward the world. The *Pastoral Constitution on the Church in the Modern World* had stated: "The joy and hope, the grief and anguish of the men of our time, especially of those who are poor or afflicted in any way, are the joy and hope, the grief and anguish of the followers of Christ as well. Nothing that is genuinely human fails to find an echo in their hearts."[22] The changed relationship to the world was also found in the council's attitude toward religious freedom, toward the other branches of Christianity, and toward other world religions. It was shown in the council's recognition "that the church, too, was part of the movement and sometimes even the drift of history." The council, or so it was thought, "put an end to the easy recourse of condemning the world as an excuse for the church to hide out in its many thick-walled fortresses." Yet, the church/world dichotomy kept popping up in the 1980s: at the 1985 synod, in numerous church documents, and at the 1989 meeting of Mexican archbishops and Vatican officials. On both sides of the church/world relationship, the language, said Steinfels, had grown "steadily more implausible" in a revival of the sinless church/sinful world dichotomy:

> Of the world we are told that it is a sinkhole of materialism, individualism, consumerism, or collectivism (depending on your economic system) and relativism. Now American culture, to start at home, has its problems—no news to readers of *Commonweal* and *America*—but to hear the Curia and our archbishops in Rome, one would think it on the verge of unredeemable depravity. Frankly I think our archbishops chose to avoid uncomfortable disagreements with their Vatican confreres by bad-mouthing the party that wasn't there to defend itself.

Steinfels agreed that it was perhaps arguable that the council had not been as critical of the world as it might have been and had regarded the world too benignly. But was that not also the council's approach to the record of the church? She noted historian John T. Noonan's remark about how "less than straightforwardly" the council had dealt with the church's historical performance on religious liberty: "Although in the life of the people of God in its pilgrimage through the vicissitudes of human history there has at times appeared a form of behavior which was hardly in keeping with the spirit of the Gospel and was even opposed to it, it has always remained the teaching of the church that no one is to be coerced into believing."[23]

If it was wise to adopt an attitude of tougher criticism toward the world, wouldn't equity demand a critical stance toward the church too? Instead, one found an energetic deemphasis on the harsher aspects of the church's record, and it was here that the plausibility crisis loomed even larger. With a note of irony she continued:

> As we are all supposed to know, the church has always taught what it teaches now: about race, about women, about slavery, about economic justice, about human rights, about torture, about who is and who is not saved. Individuals may and do err, of course, and need to repent. But magically the church need not repent: not in Germany or Spain or Austria in the 1930s and 1940s; not for the "Syllabus of Errors," or the Crusades, or the burning of heretics.

Behind the revival of the sinless church/sinful world dichotomy was "a failure of nerve," an unwillingness to trust the guidance of the spirit in a free and open conversation. "Today, instead of confronting this fear at the heart of its self-understanding, the church is garbing its own reversal, its turn away from dialogue with the declaration that it is 'countercultural.' " The countercultural label had been seized as a way of foreclosing dialogue. Noting the origin of the term as a label for the cultural revolt of the 1960s, the *Commonweal* editor commented: "As a 1960s phenomenon the counterculture usually suffered from the illusion that it did not depend upon and carry within itself most of the major traits, including some highly destructive ones, of the culture it so readily prided itself on countering. The pertinent question is this: which things are we to counter and deplore, which things to honor and cherish? . . . Dialogue rests on both a willingness to learn from the other and a humility about oneself and one's own ambiguous tradition."

Steinfels had argued that a look at the issues of gender, authority, and church and world found the gap between words and reality growing wider, where rather than confronting the crisis of language, truth, and overall direction for Catholicism and its public life, there was a tendency to settle on certain catch phrases that obscured and evaded rather than opened a critically needed examination.

Steinfels felt there were a number of reactions to this predicament, each in its own way understandable. One was simple fulmination. Many of the letters in *National Catholic Reporter* exemplified this. "Exasperation, indignation and bitterness have removed all sense of proportion. Matthew Fox is Galileo, Cardinal Ratzinger is Torquemada." This type of language too was part of the plausibility crisis. But exasperation, even with its accompanying exaggeration, was better than indifference, according to Steinfels. A second reaction was disengagement, "a gradual withering of identification with the church." Steinfels felt that Catholicism had not yet begun to measure the toll of growing indifference, particularly among the young, that the plausibility crisis was taking. Another reaction was circumscription, a narrowing of the church down to a particular parish, a particular movement or project. A fourth reaction was exile in other Christian communities. While church officials had expressed grave worries about the inroads of Pentecostalism among Hispanics, Steinfels wondered who was keeping track of the fourth-and fifth-generation Irish-, German-, and Italian-Americans, many of whom were sometimes very well educated in their faith who were finding congenial and sacramental homes within the Eastern Orthodox, the Episcopal, and the Lutheran churches? And what of the women whose desire to be of service to the church had ultimately been more welcomed in other Christian denominations?

But the reaction that was central to Steinfels's concern was "accommodation to Rome while turning a blind eye to the needs of the local church." If what she called the "centrist leadership" of the American Catholic church had any common approach to the current crisis, this was it. Among the factors entering their judgment: an ingrained deference to the Vatican, an immoderate fear of confrontation and a belief that it would only make the situation worse, and an unwritten rule that disagreement and conflict must always be contained within their own ranks and kept behind closed doors.

No one, said Steinfels, could say with complete certainty what was the prudent, wise, and pastoral and Christian response to this crisis. What would be the result of really engaging with no dissemblance the challenge of this pivotal crisis? Not all would be in equal jeopardy; bishops and archbishops might be summoned for interrogation, priests might be threatened with loss of their teaching authority or their priestly faculties, religious might be threatened with silencing and dismissed from their communities. For everyone, there would be a price to pay.

A church that lived through Vatican II and then backs away from it may end up more badly wounded than if the council had never occurred. The church itself has taught us too much about the demands of human dignity to expect a return to the preconciliar model of patient submission with the pious hope of future rehabilitation.

Steinfels said her major concern was that in mapping the course and choosing words, some in the Catholic community might misjudge the gravity of the moment and underestimate the price already being paid in demoralization, rancor, and loss of faith, all because words and deeds have parted company. "What we need are words that do not veil intentions but disclose realities. What we need," she concluded, "are candor and courage."[24]

11

Ending the Eighties

The rapid changes in Eastern Europe, the subtlety of the language of racism, and the new context of the abortion debate were among the striking themes in *Commonweal* during the last months of the 1980s.

The autumn of 1989, more abruptly than anyone might have dared to hope, brought unprecedented change throughout Eastern Europe. Fifty years after the outbreak of World War II, the international order produced by that tragic conflict was almost daily transformed. Events in Poland, Hungary, East Germany—indeed, throughout Eastern Europe—constituted "an astonishing pattern of peaceful change in one of the world's most rigidly controlled and dangerous regions," said Bryan Hehir in his *Commonweal* column. Hehir found wisdom in the apostolic letter of Pope John Paul II, written on the fiftieth anniversary of the beginning of World War II, pointing out the double challenge for the international order in the 1990s. The first challenge was to move creatively beyond the Cold War. The second challenge was to do this in a way that authentically served the welfare of the small nations of the world. Hehir said that the sense of hope that ran through East-West discussions was seldom reflected in

North-South questions of debt, development, and persistent internal or regional conflict. Hehir shared the papal view that the full potential of the moment should be seized.[1]

The most symbolic event in all the series of rapid changes was the Berlin wall. *Commonweal* noted the symbolic role the wall had played "in the cold war; in cementing the alliance of Western Europe and the U.S.; in the iconography of division, destruction and nuclear threat."[2] *Commonweal's* correspondent, Czarina Wilpert, reported that some described the November 9, 1989, piercing of the wall as the time when the *Volkspolizei* (the East German "peoples' police") learned to smile. "It was truly strange to see those cold stares turn to smiles," wrote Wilpert.[3] Both *Commonweal* and its reporter shared the sense of joy and liberation, but also the sense of challenge for a peaceful and democratic evolution in Germany, Eastern Europe, and the Soviet Union.

African-Americans

It was Edward K. Braxton, a priest in the archdiocese of Chicago and an author of many articles on African-American Catholics, who raised the issue in *Commonweal* of the subtle racism that was often implicit, even if unintentional, in the way the words *minority* and *minority groups* were used. Ordinarily, minority meant that one group consisted of fewer members than another group whose larger numbers constituted the majority. When used in reference to race and ethnicity, however, the word became subtly shaded. In the U.S. the term *minorities* was presumed to refer primarily to certain groups: people of African, Hispanic, or Asian origins. Oddly, it was rarely used to refer to other groups, such as Jewish or Japanese people, though the size of those groups was far smaller than the African-American population. Why was it that these groups were not referred to as minorities? Because, Braxton concluded, the word *minority* was a loaded term, associated with a host of problems: poverty, illiteracy, unemployment, drugs, violence, and unwed parents. Thus, a story about minorities in America can easily evoke images, said Braxton, "of a group that is weak, passive and inferior, lacking self-determination, possessing little that others desire, and having few resources for solving its own problems." The majority group, on the other hand, "is strong, active, self-determining, possessing what others need and want, and having the resources for solving its problems." The frequent use of the term *minority group* in reference to black Americans could be a tragic reenforcement of the status quo. Used by blacks themselves, it could become a self-fulfilling prophecy.

The word *blacks* does not link people of African descent to a larger group or history beyond the United States. On the other hand, the term *African-American* can help black people in the United States to become more conscious of their historical and racial links with over 600 million people throughout the world who have Africa as their genesis. This might go a long way in combating the negative connotations that are almost immediately associated with the expression *minority group*. The world is multiracial, and whites do not constitute the majority of the world's population. The eventual banishment of the problematic use of the term *minority*, said Braxton, could "challenge all people not to focus attention on who and what people are not, but on who and what they are."[4]

While such questions of language change and attitudinal change continued, Spike Lee's provocative film *Do the Right Thing* brought the sensitive theme of racial antagonism—long suppressed in American life—to the forefront. The film's plot centered on a Bedford-Stuyvesant pizzeria owned by a middle-aged Italian-American (Danny Aiello), who has refused to leave the decaying area despite his son's pleas. Spike Lee (wearing an old Brooklyn Dodgers' shirt with Jackie Robinson's number) plays the store's deliveryman. The film was extremely frank about racial prejudice, not just between white and black but also between black and Latino, black and Asian, and others. *Commonweal* critic Tom O'Brien noted one sequence in the film that involved "a set of expletives directed at everyone, so universal and absurd that it both disgusts and amuses." He felt the film was more successful at raising issues than resolving them, but that it was, nevertheless, worthwhile and timely. The real-life lack of frank discourse had not been helpful. Conservatives "haven't wanted to hear such discourse," he asserted, and liberals were often "too polite to face all the issues." This had produced "a benign neglect of black and white tensions on screen for almost two decades."[5] Another *Commonweal* contributor found the film "wacky and wildly disturbing," especially in its searing last image, a quote from Malcolm X that seemed to endorse the violence portrayed on the screen.[6] Yet another contributor pointed out that the Malcolm X quote was not representative of his final thoughts on violence, and that "in some ways his death at the hands of Black Muslim henchmen was caused by his espousal of nonviolence as well as his disaffection for Elijah Muhammed's Nation of Islam."[7]

Abortion

On July 3, 1989, in *Webster v. Reproductive Health Services*, the Supreme Court upheld a Missouri law that permitted testing for fetal viability at twenty weeks of pregnancy and prohibited any use of public facilities or public employees for abortion. Almost without exception, Court decisions since *Roe v. Wade* in 1973 had overturned restrictions on abortion. With *Webster*, it appeared that a new direction had emerged.

Commonweal was "not so sure," as the Court had not dismantled *Roe*, and furthermore, whatever the law, there was an abortion ethic very deeply rooted in American culture. A change in law would mean little without a transformation of minds and hearts. While one might argue that *Roe* had engendered the abortion ethic—"this unique exception to our general prohibition of killing innocent others"—it was difficult to find in the *Roe* decision itself the absolutist language that had increasingly taken over. For example, "abortion on demand" and "the absolute right to privacy" had become catchphrases. But back in 1973, the Court had written: "Appellants . . . argue that the woman's right is absolute and that she is entitled to terminate her pregnancy at whatever time, in whatever way, and for whatever reason she alone chooses. With this we do not agree." The Court went on: "The right of personal privacy includes the abortion decision, but . . . this right is not unqualified and must be considered against important state interests in regulation." *Commonweal* felt it was not hard for the Court to find justification in these words for upholding the Missouri law. The editors were wary of the acrimonious scramble for influence in fifty state houses that *Webster* had likely ushered in, but they held the hope that the coming political struggle could be built on the sense that one-and-a-half million abortions a year were too many and that women and fetuses alike were "victims of a shabby ethic."[8]

The editors asked ten knowledgeable observers (five men and five women) to comment briefly on the *Webster* decision. Moral theologian Richard McCormick, S. J., expressed frustration because *Webster* had moved against *Roe* "in a technical, chip-away manner that promises to leave us preoccupied in the months ahead with single-issue politics, scare tactics, worn-out rhetoric, and a disastrous neglect of other social and even prolife concerns." For Mary Ann Glendon, professor of law at Harvard and author of *Abortion and Divorce in Western Law*, the decision affirmed "the right of Americans to have important issues decided by majoritarian political processes except when these have been clearly removed from the legislative purview by constitutional text or tradition." Political scientist Fred Siegel felt that among pro-life and pro-choice organizations, the side that showed the most tactical flexibility in reaching out to "the great mass of the public that supports neither of their positions" had the best chance of winning politically. The most provocative remark of any of the ten commentators—who ranged from hot and cold to neutral on *Webster*—belonged to pro-choicer Daniel Callahan. Callahan, the former *Commonweal* editor who has dealt with abortion in his scholarly work since the 1960s, thought that, in the long run, a more restrictive set of abortion laws might have a greater chance of permanent endurance.[9]

Four months after *Webster*, *Commonweal* wrote that the great political and moral debate that was promised (and in some quarters dreaded) following the Court's decision in July still eluded the nation. The National Abortion Rights Action League (NARAL) had managed "to turn the focus on our national antipathy toward politicians." With the slogan "Who decides? women or politicians?," NARAL was playing hard to "the visceral antipathy among Americans to government interference in their lives." The liberal-left pro-choicers' recourse to a get-government-off-our-backs strategy was, said *Commonweal*, only one of the political ironies leading us astray.

The National Right to Life Committee's efforts to introduce more restrictive laws at the state level seemed to have been eclipsed by Operation Rescue, whose members blocked abortion clinics in the face of court orders, jail sentences, and crushing fines. The mainstream pro-life movement kept a careful distance from Operation Rescue and its disruptive tactics. There was thus a special irony in the possibility that by drawing on methods carefully honed by liberals and leftists in the civil rights and anti-Vietnam movements, Operation Rescue might evoke fears and general reactions that would "completely derail any hope for reaching legislative compromises on the abortion issue."

But most disheartening to *Commonweal* was the failure of politicians to demonstrate the moral and political seriousness that the abortion issue required. *Commonweal's* editorial "The Politics of Evasion," written by Peggy Steinfels, expressed particular disappointment with Governor Mario Cuomo of New York. Before *Webster*, she pointed out, it could be argued, as the governor had, that abortion on demand was "the law of the land" and that as a public official he had to uphold the law embodied in *Roe*. Though *Webster* had not withdrawn the right established in *Roe*, it had finally acknowledged what was also stated in *Roe*—that the state may have an interest in the protection of a viable fetus in the third trimester. The fetus now had an acknowledged standing in the legal arena, and abortion on demand, noted Steinfels, need no longer be the only law of the land. In the death penalty debate, she argued, Governor Cuomo had "used his powers of discernment and eloquence in an attempt to move the citizenry toward his own views opposing capital punishment, views based on moral as well as political principles." *Commonweal* regretted that at this juncture in the national abortion debate, the governor seemed "to stand back from using those considerable talents to engage the body politic in considering the value of developing human life." He was one of those political leaders who, rather than engaging in the debate, seemed "to be evading it."[10]

As the discussion continued both in *Commonweal* and in the nation, Cuomo did join the debate with a two-thousand-word contribution to the correspondence section of the magazine. He said that while he shared the editors' dismay at the number of abortions, he felt that *Webster* had not introduced any fundamental legal change. On the alleged inconsistency between his positions on abortion and the death penalty, he maintained that if he judged that theoretically doable legal restrictions on abortion were fair and would engender a greater respect for life, then he would have to be disposed to advocate for such change, and if he judged that the imposition of the death penalty would save innocent lives and make the state a safer and better place, then he would have to support that penalty. In fact, in each case his "prudential political judgment" was that these actions would not have such desirable effects and would more likely "merely enable us to ignore the root causes of abortion and crime, and soothe our consciences by allowing us to believe we had done everything possible when we had brought the coercive power of the law to bear." He said he felt gratitude that the Catholic bishops had contributed to keeping abortion from becoming a nonissue, "something that does not deserve and demand our attention." He also felt that while one should not and did not expect bishops to be politicians, neither should one "exempt them from the demands of prudence in the political arena." Referring to Bishop Leo Maher of San Diego, who had barred a Catholic pro-choice candidate for the California legislature from receiving communion, and the resultant publicity and reaction, Cuomo said: "When the public perception is that they are not simply exercising their teaching role for Catholics, but trying to influence the outcome of an election, there will be publicity." Of the Maher affair, *Commonweal* agreed: "Americans may be troubled about voting against fetuses, but they have no compunction about voting against religious authority-figures who seem to push themselves unwarrantedly into the political arena—and that goes for Catholics."[11] The governor and *Commonweal* also came together regarding Bishop Austin Vaughan of New York, who had stated that Cuomo had put himself "at serious risk of going to hell" because of his position on abortion and public policy. Said *Commonweal*: "Bishops have a responsibility to teach and even to enforce the moral law; but their office does not confer the power to read souls, or to make apodictic judgments about how a particular moral principle is to be translated into law and public policy."[12] Said Cuomo: "Amen." He closed his lengthy letter with the hope that *Commonweal* would see that he was not "ducking for cover" on the abortion issue.[13]

The Cuomo letter to *Commonweal* was itself given extensive press attention, but, as *Commonweal* pointed out, with the exception of the reports in *Washington Post*, the press coverage highlighted "the low tolerance of most reporters for serious discussion of the abortion question and the pro-choice bias of New York newspapers." *Commonweal's* response to the letter extended the discussion with Cuomo on such subjects as regarding parental notification, viability testing, and counseling and praised him for doing "more than some of his critics to keep abortion from being treated as a settled question." The editors' "chief disappointment" with his response, however, was that he had not stepped forth as a molder of consensus. Turning to the famous debate between Abraham Lincoln and Senator Stephen Douglas over the 1857 Dred Scott decision, they quoted Lincoln: "He who moulds public sentiment goes deeper than he who enacts statutes or pronounces decisions. He makes statutes and decisions possible or impossible to be executed." Cuomo, they felt, possessed Lincoln-like oratorical skills and had already demonstrated an ability to link moral wisdom with rhetorical power, and they clearly wanted, and hoped for, more from him on abortion. As in 1857, so in 1990. The political culture was "caught up in a fierce struggle over whether some human lives can be placed beyond the protection of the law."[14]

12

Sixty-fifth Anniversary

"As anniversaries go, sixty-fifths rank third; quarters and halves of centuries count for more." So noted *Commonweal*, as it introduced its sixty-fifth anniversary issue, November 17, 1989. The contents of the issue were, however, clearly of the first order. Observers more detached than publisher Edward Skillin would nonetheless agree with him that on the basis of the anniversary issue, *Commonweal* was "at its all time best," and the octogenarian Skillin added, "the sixty-fifth anniversary is a harbinger of a great future."[1]

There were three essays. In a critical analysis that was both historical and contemporary, "Join It, Work It, Fight It: American Catholics and the American Way," David J. O'Brien explored the styles of public presence of Catholicism.[2] In "Preaching the Word and Doing It: Black Catholics in America," Albert Raboteau showed how crucial African-American Catholics were to the history of America and drew some important lessons from this for the identity and religious vigor of the community.[3] In "Getting Our Heads Together: An Agenda for Catholic Intellectuals," Sidney Callahan analyzed the responsibilities and difficulties faced by intellectuals in general, and Catholic intellectuals in particular, in a role she

characterized as the "intelligence service of the society."[4]

In addition, the issue featured ten perspectives on the challenges facing U.S. Catholics in the years ahead to 2000.[5] While acknowledging the importance of other issues, such as equal rights for women—including the ordination of women—Father Andrew Greeley believed that improving the quality of preaching was the church's biggest challenge.

> For most Catholics the church is their parish. Their main contact with the parish is the weekend liturgy and the principal exchange between priest and people is the homily. Research evidence shows that the quality of Sunday preaching is the strongest predictor of strength of affiliation with the church, after the religious behavior of the spouse. Yet most American Catholics gave their priests very poor grades on what they consider to be priests' most important role.

Greeley felt that "the laity must demand good preaching."[6]

Kenneth Woodward, a senior writer for *Newsweek*, saw a greater challenge upon which he, he felt, serious Catholics of all ideological bents could agree. It was the same challenge the church had "failed to meet in the 1980s and 1970s: passing on the faith and traditions to the next generations."

> To grow up Catholic, you first have to grow up. In this society, at any rate, I see the young captured by a vapid, boring, commercialized youth culture and not interested in becoming adults. Someone has to show them that adulthood requires character and commitment. Friendship, sex, education, work, creativity, family—these experiences that the young say they want don't just happen. They must be recognized, anticipated, worked for, prized.

Woodward's point was not to put down the young, but to encourage parents, teachers, parish workers, clergy, and hierarchy to get the message across to young people that "to be a Catholic is to be different, certainly different from what the media and malls of the youth culture tell them to be." What struck Woodward most about Catholics between fifteen and thirty was not only how little they knew about their faith but also how much they failed to recognize "that, among other things, Christianity offers a critique of their own society and culture."[7]

For Georgetown University theologian Monika K. Hellwig, the greatest challenge was "whether we can put ordinary Catholic believers in touch with . . . their heritage in ways that will make the fullness of the heritage their own."

> As I have been able to observe what is going on, there is a small minority of Catholics who are both intellectually curious about their tradition and wholeheartedly committed to it, but there is a large majority who are vaguely holding on and waiting for something more to happen which will make sense of their own fidelity.

Hellwig found her Catholic identity "by looking along a historical axis for continuity and consistency in the midst of change." She worried, however, that ordinary Catholics, unspecialized in theology or church history, had not been provided the resources with which they might make such discoveries of continuity for themselves. "What they tend to see is discontinuity," wrote Hellwig. "They may be concerned about it and resist all changes indiscriminately and tend to lose their sense of direction."[8]

Author George Weigel addressed a similar theme. Said Weigel: "I believe we are called to the recovery and extension of a distinctive Catholic identity: the fundamental prerequisite to evangelization and service." He felt there had been an "obsession" with the question of authority in the church and that this must give way "to a new quest for what is authoritative in our lives: authoritative in terms of the Gospel, and authoritative in terms of the living tradition of the church."

Catholic deconstructionists and Catholic "restorationists" alike have missed the crucial truth in Jaroslav Pelikan's definition of "tradition" as the living faith of those who have gone before. Deconstructionists who dismiss Paul, Augustine and the Cappadocian Fathers as impossibly sexist, and restorationists who identify "tradition" with practices about as ancient as our great-grandmothers, have both done a lot of damage to a sense of Catholic identity.[9]

Commonweal's editorial for its sixty-fifth anniversary issue reflected on the magazine's history and responsibility to bring "a religious perspective to 'the great issues of the day,' . . . and a worldly perspective to the great issues of the church." On both sides of the church-world equation the editors found an "established disorder" that was often disheartening. But they were grateful that *Commonweal's* independence and dual perspective had allowed both readers and editors to express "a deep commitment to and a deep discontent with the church and the society in which the church has ultimately flourished." They spoke of the standards that the best of the Catholic tradition espoused for a civil society: the social nature of human beings, the rights and responsibilities of human beings within an attentive community, and the reasoned discourse that governs and sustains such communities through a vigorous politics. These standards, they maintained, also constituted "the threads of argument that have woven their way through *Commonweal's* sixty-five years." They affirmed the need for such criteria of community and justice in a society that often exhibited a paralyzed politics, brittle culture, and mean-spirited public life. They praised Pope John Paul II's encyclical *On Social Concerns* for providing "a framework for analyzing the moral choices now to be faced in the disintegration of the Soviet empire, the reduction in East-West tensions, and the growing gap in economic resources between North and South." They also praised elements of social teaching by U. S. bishops that revealed an acute moral insight. They found it paradoxical, however, that such well-honed skills, rigorous moral analysis, and urgent calls for justice should elude the pope and bishops "when it comes to the life of the church itself." The great expectations following Vatican II had, after twenty-five years, come up against "a social barrier of fear and insecurity, created to a large degree . . . by Roman overreaching and highhandedness." Informed laity and clergy had heard from some local bishops whispers of "how difficult a time it is and that patience is the order of the day." *Commonweal* felt there was something to be said for this. "But only something. And only temporarily." They quoted the words of the usually moderate London *Tablet* that much that went under the name "discretion" in the contemporary church was a cover "for what is in fact sheer spinelessness."[10]

Commonweal argued that the laity must come to see that the future of the Catholic church is their responsibility and must act in accord with this belief. The contents of the sixty-fifth anniversary issue could be seen as an agenda for this responsibility. Among the themes that the editors insisted must be addressed were

> concern for the future of faithfulness, especially but not only among the younger members of the people of God; need for a more authentic expression of our incarnational theology, linking the life of faith to our work in the world, yearning for a distinctive Catholic, sensibility in the midst of a bourgeois culture.

Clearly, there was much more to be done. The editorial concluded with a one-word statement, without exclamation, but with declarative determination and a faith-filled resoluteness: "Onward."[11]

Conclusions: A Very Worthy Conversation

At a conference on the Catholic church and American culture, Peggy Steinfels, in 1988, described her understanding of *Commonweal's* identity. Her audience was largely composed of presidents of Catholic colleges and universities who themselves had a keen interest in questions dealing with the life of Catholic intellectual communities and institutions. She described *Commonweal* as "a very small institution" that operated on certain basic assumptions:

1. ideas count;
2. being Catholic counts;
3. the way we shape our ideas, connect and disconnect them from one another, reject and accept them, are deeply tied, are central to the story we tell ourselves about what it means to be an American Catholic.

She spoke of the seriousness of Catholic identity and warned against the tendency of some to abandon this identity. "Every time a staff opening is announced at *Commonweal*, the magazine has been approached by people, Catholic and non-Catholic, who think an explicitly Catholic journal is out of date." She felt, however, that the tendency to deny or downplay Catholic identity had an equally unfortunate counter-tendency in "the assertion of Catholic identity by reverting to a vicious cycle of authoritarianism . . . or by insisting that Catholic identity consists in a blind identification with what some conservative groups call papal orthodoxy."

Steinfels maintained that *Commonweal's* identity was based on a long and rich Catholic tradition, on the particular history of the magazine itself, and on its response to present conditions. Becoming a *Commonweal* editor meant joining a magazine that has a sixty-five-year tradition of being a journal of public affairs, religion, literature, and the arts edited by Roman Catholic laypeople. "In continuing that tradition I have a two-part task: first to honestly try to understand the facts of the matter, be they third world debt, the pope's newest encyclical, or public education; second, to draw on *Commonweal's* Catholic tradition and our own understanding of Catholicism to frame and interpret those facts." *Commonweal* is "a bridge for a two-way conversation between faith and life; my job is to continue that conversation."[1]

Having now attended to that ongoing conversation from the 1970s to the 1990s, let us draw a few conclusions from it.

1

Commonweal has sustained an extensive, articulate, and inclusive conversation on abortion and has done so while masking nothing and conveying deep moral seriousness.

It is not by chance that the most extensive treatment of any theme in our study has been the abortion issue. Nor is it by chance that the longest single article in *Commonweal's* history was the debate between Daniel C. Maguire and James Burtchaell.[2] One recalls also the extensive discussion regarding *Commonweal's* editorial "Do Catholics Have Constitutional Rights?"[3] Participants included the *Nation,* the *Wall Street Journal,* the American Civil Liberties Union, Planned Parenthood, Richard Neuhaus, Henry Hyde, Leo Pfeffer, and others.

Perhaps it is notable that both Peter and Peggy Steinfels worked with the Hastings Center before coming to *Commonweal* full-time. The center is a secular think tank for issues of society, ethics, and the life sciences. But *Commonweal's* editorial concern with abortion predates the presence of either of the Steinfels. Nonetheless, both have been very articulate. Peter's work has already been well reported, but consider this passage from a 1990 editorial, as an example of Peggy's influence:

> The original women's movement was in part an angry, and justified, protest against patriarchal and chauvinist abuses, large and small. On its positive side it projected a vision of a more egalitarian society, one in which rights and responsibilities mutu-

ally reinforce and sustain one another. The insistence of NOW and NARAL and their allies on an unqualified right of abortion signals the loss of that vision and something more. That insistence is on the brink of implanting another moral norm altogether. It goes as follows: The right to abortion will be and should be absolute because women are and always will be victims. Victims are exempt from the reciprocity that makes the interplay of rights and responsibilities possible. Victims need not abide by the rule that says I will treat others as I would wish to be treated. . . . Is this what the women's movement is to become?

The editorial goes on to assess the Catholic church with the same candid approach:

The Catholic church has taken a drubbing, some of it justified, over the abortion issue. *Humanae vitae,* and the fall-into-line response it evoked from the world's hierarchy, tore holes in the church's credibility on sex-related morality. The gender bias built into the church's command-and-control structure doesn't help. On abortion itself, the church has lost respect through the words and actions of a few bishops, the tactics used by some in Operation Rescue, a simplistic readiness on the part of some church leaders to endorse single-issue politics as an acceptable means of halting the abortion tide.

But the more basic reason for Catholic-bashing these days has to do not with the maladroit use of dubious tactics but with something more basic: the bishops identify abortion as the taking of human life, and they say it is wrong. They ask us, including the politicians among us to examine the ingredients on the "choice" label and consider whether ingesting this stew is good for the moral health of the community.

The editorial goes on to challenge an op-ed piece by Arthur Schlesinger, Jr., in the *New York Times* and concludes with the exhortation that elicited the two-thousand-word response noted earlier from Governor Mario Cuomo.[4]

The conversation on abortion continues with vigor in *Commonweal.*

2
Commonweal has sustained an articulate and inclusive conversation on the Roman Catholic church and its life and practice in the modern world.

Were it not for *Commonweal* one would not have been able to see the convergence of thinking of John Deedy, Monika K. Hellwig, Ken Woodward, and George Weigel as they reflected on the challenges facing Catholics in the next decade in the magazine's sixty-fifth anniversary symposium. Nor would one have been able to encounter side by side the thoughts of Sister Theresa Kane, Father Andrew Greeley, Cardinal John O'Connor, and Abigail McCarthy.[5]

Of similar uniqueness was *Commonweal's* symposium that culminated with the excellent series "From the Council to the Synod." Once again, only the pages of *Commonweal* could bring into conversation the thinking of Garry Wills, Jean Vanier, J. Peter Grace, Mary Gordon, Mary Durkin, Tom Fox, Joseph Sobran, and others.[6] The series of articles preceding the symposium, which featured the work of such authors as Avery Dulles, Gregory Baum, Elisabeth Schussler Fiorenza, and Joseph Komonchak, was also distinguished.[7]

While these were special issues, the regular contributions of columnists and book reviewers must also be mentioned. John Garvey has won the Catholic Press Association prize for best column for so many years that former editor David Toolan, now at *America,* says it should simply be called the Garvey Trophy.[8] Likewise, the review section has regularly been lauded, a section Toolan himself edited for ten years. As one citation put it: "No other publication equals *Commonweal* in the depth and professionalism of its review sections."[9] Editorials, also with a very long string of prizes, have been duly noted already in our study, but letters were also important. Letters have been a very worthy part of the splendid conversation in *Commonweal.*

3
Commonweal *has sustained a conversation characterized by a tradition of civility, fairmindedness,
and vigor.*

The wide range of participants in the conversation in *Commonweal* is itself testimony to this. Veteran readers know and
appreciate the *Commonweal* style. The most notable lapse
was with some essentially superficial aspects of Peter
Steinfels's "Michael Novak and His Ultrasuper Democraticapitalism."[10] One might be either outraged or amused by such
cleverness with one-liners, but either way, this was not the
Commonweal style. Bernard Murchland, a reader and an occasional author in *Commonweal* for many years, found some
"ritualistic dumping on Novak" but also "some confessional
humility" in what was essentially a very serious and important
essay.[11] It is also worth noting that a 1984 *Commonweal* editorial on reconciliation extended its hand to Novak,[12] who has
since been an occasional contributor in recent years.

That we need to search hard to find something at odds
with *Commonweal*'s history of civility and fairmindedness is a
further witness to this tradition. Another aspect of this tradition is the spirit of seriousness and rigor in which the magazine is edited. Peggy Steinfels comments:

> *Commonweal* editors read hundreds of manuscripts
> a year. That we agree on rejecting so many and
> accepting so few means we share a standard about
> what fits the magazine's tradition as well as a stan-
> dard about what is intelligent, helpful, informative,
> moving writing, and what is not. We look for hon-
> esty and clarity of expression. We distinguish moral-
> izing from moral analysis; church talk and liberal
> cant from real language; empty phrases from ones
> filled with meaning.

She humbly admits that "sometimes we fail."[13] Perhaps, but
not very often. The tradition of rigor, fairmindedness, and
civility is what continues to make the *Commonweal* conversation unique.

4

*The conversation in **Commonweal** frequently has been at the cutting edge of the creative inculturation of Catholicism in the United States.*

Commonweal has no monopoly on this, of course. In her address to the college presidents, Peggy Steinfels exhorted them to the challenge of the creative inculturation of Catholicism in the United States:

> See yourselves for what you are, Catholic colleges and universities that are a public resource, critical to the task of carrying on a coherent conversation about church and world, faith and life, ethics and the workplace; of establishing the links between knowledge and justice . . . to make sense of what is a fragmented culture.[14]

The task of relating to the culture in both an appreciative and critical way is one that has been at the center of *Commonweal's* identity since the earliest days of the magazine. This was the theme of a 1925 series of articles "Obligations to America," written by the distinguished historian Carlton J. Hayes. Reprinted in pamphlet form, these articles provided a virtual platform for the early *Commonweal*.[15] The sixty-fifth anniversary issue continued with this theme, especially David J. O'Brien's essay "Join It, Work It, Fight It: American Catholics and the American Way."[16]

Some Catholics have always understood that Catholicism not only contributes to American culture but also that Catholicism can learn from it. The first American bishop, John Carroll, knew that, and Pope John Paul II has understood inculturation, at least in principle, in a way that brings out the idea of reciprocity.[17] At the time of *Commonweal's* founding, historian Peter Guilday wrote privately of the "glorious mission" that *Commonweal* had to inspire in Catholics a spirit of critical service to both country and church. He felt there was "talent aplenty in the land," but he was doubtful there would be "much courage in dealing with American Church matters." He seemed to even doubt himself. "If the review manages to give the little fellows like me just that peculiar drop of ambrosial confidence . . . it will be a blessing. I don't want it to take me up off my knees but I do want it to put some gumption into my prayers."[18] Over the years, *Commonweal* has conveyed both a sense of prayerful faithfulness and a sense of gumption. This attitude has characterized *Commonweal*'s stance toward both its faith and its country. As John Garvey put it, "*Commonweal* has shown an uncommon knack for being at the forefront of American Catholic thought."[19] In the sixty-fifth anniversary issue, writer George Weigel noted the spirit of cultural reciprocity and creative inculturation that is fundamental to Catholicism and, we might add, to *Commonweal*'s mission. Weigel suggests the need for contemporary Catholicism to follow the example of three great figures of American Catholic history: John Carroll, Isaac Hecker, and James Gibbons.

> Each of these men understood that the universality of Catholic truth took on a particularly dynamic expression when mediated through the distinctive experience of being American. Each knew that Rome had much to teach America, and that America had things to teach its elder sister on the Tiber. Each lived, in sum, a creative tension between universality and particularity, by incarnating the classic Catholic tradition in a distinctively American way.[20]

The spirit of quest for the creative inculturation of Catholicism in America, both learning from the culture and contributing positively and critically to it and to the church, is truly the history of *Commonweal*. The history of this quest runs from Carlton Hayes to David O'Brien, from Peter Guilday to George Weigel. It is present through a long succession of *Commonweal* editors that clearly includes current editor Peggy Steinfels. It is the quest for *being Catholic*.

   In the introduction to this book, it was pointed out that the earlier study of *Commonweal*'s first fifty years indicated that the magazine had recapitulated the broad outline of the history of Catholics in the United States. Each had followed a historical evolution from what might in one sense be called patrician origins through immigrant Catholic coming-of-age to maturity and identity crisis. This parallel pattern has continued through the past two decades. Catholicism in the United States has presented notable signs of its creative inculturation. The two pastoral letters *The Challenge of Peace* and *Economic Justice for All* were obvious signs of this. Each letter was both appreciative and critical of dimensions of the American experience. Each letter revealed a Catholicism in mature, confident, and respectfully open dialogue with a pluralistic culture that, at the same time, did not simply want to assimilate into the culture but rather wished to fulfill its responsibilities for transforming the culture. Arij Roest Crollius, who has written extensively on inculturation, describes three stages in the process: translation, assimilation, and transformation.[21] Clearly, Catholicism in the United States shows major signs of being in the third stage. In 1959, John Cogley criticized American Catholics: "We content ourselves with standing in judgment on our age as if *its* problems were not our problems, as if *its* failures were not our own, as if the challenges confronting *it* were not confronting us."[22] No informed observer would say this of Catholicism today.

Gerald P. Fogarty, the respected Jesuit historian, has noted that Rome's condemnation of Americanism in 1899 brought with it an authoritarian spirit and discipline that resulted in a "stifling of intellectual life." With the condemnation of modernism following so closely on the condemnation of Americanism, "the American Catholic Church," wrote Fogarty, "lapsed into an intellectual slumber from which it did not awaken until the 1940s."[23] *Commonweal*, however, largely through the influence of the remarkable George N. Shuster, began an awakening from its first issue in 1924. In one sense its mission of seeking the creative inculturation of Catholicism in America was continuous. In the 1960s, the American Catholic church felt the exhilaration of Pope John XXIII, the Kennedy presidency, and the satisfaction of seeing much that it had long sought ratified in Vatican II. But it also knew the traumas of big mistakes for America in Vietnam and big mistakes for the church in *Humanae Vitae*. Being chastened in both their American and Catholic identity, however, did not mean giving up on either of these. The critical and appreciative dimensions of its mission of creative inculturation proceeded ever more effectively. *Commonweal* and the corps of critical reflective intelligence it convened in conversation, even though challenged and undercut more often than served by a Vatican moving from the Aggiornamento of Pope John XXIII to the Restoration of Pope John Paul II, has been frequently at the cutting edge of the creative inculturation of Catholicism in America. The need for the creative inculturation of Catholicism in the United States continues, as clearly does the need for *Commonweal* as an independent intellectual voice in the church that shares that commitment. *The Commonweal and American Catholicism* (Fortress, 1974) concluded by observing that, at that point in history, one would have to consider carefully the claim that *Commonweal* had "been perhaps the most important symbol and achievement of the American Catholic laity."[24] Such a claim continues to deserve careful consideration as we ponder the past and contemplate the future.

Afterword

The Unique Contribution of Edward S. Skillin to *Commonweal*

As one who has had the opportunity to research *Commonweal*'s history, both in *The Commonweal and American Catholicism*, which covered events through the 1970s, and this book, which has continued the story since then, there is one more observation that must be shared. While *Commonweal* has been created and sustained by a community, the contribution of Edward S. Skillin has been unique.

In 1924, *Commonweal*, then known as *The Commonweal*, was conceived as the flagship for Catholic intellectuals. It was brought into existence by the Calvert Associates, the group formed largely through the efforts of Michael Williams, who went from coast to coast in his fundraising and promotional efforts. Williams became *Commonweal*'s first editor. Within two years, the multitalented George N. Shuster was on board as an assistant editor. He soon became managing editor. The first fifteen years of *Commonweal* are clearly the Williams and Shuster years. In the fifty years or so since 1939, a number of editors have played important leadership roles, but the commitment of Edward Skillin has made him the *sine qua non* of *Commonweal*.

Skillin first sought to join *Commonweal* in 1925 when he graduated from Williams College, but he was turned down. After eight years with Henry Holt Publishers, and having completed an M.A. from Columbia University, he was hired by George Shuster. On April 20, 1934, he contributed the first of the more than three thousand articles, reviews, and editorials he would write over the next five-and-a-half decades. He served as coeditor from 1938 to 1947, editor from 1947 to 1967 and has served as publisher since 1967.

The Williams College *Alumni Review* for Winter 1988 contained a full-page profile of Skillin entitled "Edward Skillin '25: *Commonweal's* Guiding Force." A descriptive paragraph stated:

> In his 80s, Skillin is a vital man, small-boned and compact. His bright eyes signal high intelligence and ready wit. Above all one sees kindness in his face. Most weekdays, he jogs to early Mass, eats breakfast, and takes a train from the New Jersey suburb [Upper Montclair], where he lives with his wife and older son, to his office on Dutch Street in lower Manhattan.[1]

At the office, the Phi Beta Kappa member, who has received five honorary degrees and the 1987 St. Francis de Sales Award of the Catholic Press Association, can generally be found with a legal pad in hand. Peter Steinfels commented: "Everything computers can tell you, Edward can tell you from his yellow legal pads. He's very intelligent and a splendid record keeper." Steinfels added: "*Commonweal* has never had much money. The magazine has existed over sixty years on the brink of bankruptcy, but he always manages to pull us through."[2]

However, it is not just careful financial management nor the one-and-a-half million words he has contributed to *Commonweal's* pages nor perhaps even his four decades of editorship that have been most significant in his years at the magazine. "What Edward has contributed is best understood in the light of his way of life and way of thinking," the staff wrote in the Spring 1988 *Associates Newsletter*. "It's hard to pin down," said Peter Steinfels, "but because of Ed there's a certain spirit at *Commonweal*." Steinfels further stated that he feels that the inner life of *Commonweal's* small organization has "a sense of community and peace—largely due to Ed." Jim O'Gara noted that Skillin "never says anything uncharitable." O'Gara also recalled how Skillin's generosity to the homeless resulted in so many people coming to the office one day that Skillin finally had to put a stop to it because they were causing disruption. "After that they met him outside," said O'Gara. In 1989, Skillin and his wife Jane, responding to an item in their parish bulletin, adopted two Vietnamese youngsters, Liem, sixteen-years old, and Dinh, eighteen-years old, two refugees who escaped first from their own country and later from a camp in Malaysia.[3]

The *Commonweal* story is one that has involved great numbers of authors, reviewers, editors, associates, and subscribers. But amid all this, the manifold contribution of Edward Skillin must be recognized. Our focus in this study has been from the 1970s to the 1990s, years during which Skillin served as publisher, rather than in any editorial role. Still, one is struck by the special quality of his quiet presence and impact.[4] As the staff wrote in 1988, he is still the "keeper of the corporate conscience" and the "guardian of the institutional memory."[5]

Notes

Introduction

[1] George N. Shuster, "Fortieth Anniversary Symposium," *Commonweal*, 20 Nov. 1964, 262. See Rodger Van Allen, *The Commonweal and American Catholicism* (Philadelphia: Fortress Press, 1974), 9. *Commonweal* is hereafter cited as *Com.*

[2] The quote has been used in *Commonweal's* promotional literature and appears in *Com.*, 5 May 1989, 288.

[3] Andrew M. Greeley and Peter H. Rossi, *The Education of Catholic Americans* (Chicago: Aldine Publishing Co., 1966), 16. The *Commonweal* sample, from which clergy and religious readers were eliminated, showed that almost three-fourths had attended Catholic colleges or universities, and over one-third attended mass more than once a week.

[4] See Van Allen, 27.

Chapter 1

[1] "The Abortion Decision," *Com.*, 16 Feb. 1973, 435–36.

[2] Robert Drinan, "The Abortion Decision: The Supreme Court Balances Privacy and Pregnancy," *Com.*, 16 Feb. 1973, 438–40.

[3] Paul Ramsey, "Protecting the Unborn," *Com.*, 31 May 1974, 308–14.

[4] Daniel A. Degnan, "Laws, Morals and Abortion," *Com.*, 31 May 1974, 305–8.

[5] "Catholics and Abortion," *Com.*, 31 May 1974, 299–300.

[6] Ibid.

[7] "Trend on Views Toward Abortion," in *The Gallup Poll: Public Opinion 1981* (Wilmington, Del.: Scholarly Resources, 1982), 117–18. Also see *The Gallup Poll: Public Opinion 1986*

(Wilmington, Del.: Scholarly Resources, 1987), 51: "Support for the ruling has declined slightly since 1983."

[8] Raymond G. Decker and Walter R. Trinkaus, "The Abortion Decision: Two Years Later," *Com.*, 14 Feb. 1975, 384–90.

[9] "The New Abortion Debate," *Com.*, 22 July 1977, 451–52.

[10] Peter Steinfels, "The Politics of Abortion," *Com.*, 22 July 1977, 456.

[11] "Do Catholics Have Constitutional Rights?" *Com.*, 8 Dec. 1978, 771–73.

[12] Aryeh Neier, "Theology and the Constitution," *Nation*, 30 Dec. 1978, 722, 726–27; "A New Anti-Catholic Bigotry?" *Wall Street Journal*, 15 Dec. 1978; "Correspondence," *Com.*, 2 Feb. 1979, 34, 61–63.

[13] "Correspondence," ibid., 62–63.

[14] "Abortion, Religion and Political Life," *Com.*, 2 Feb. 1979, 35–38.

[15] *Supreme Court Reporter*, vol. 1004 (St. Paul, Minn.: West Publishing Co., 1982), 2671–72.

[16] "Abortion: A Severe Testing," *Com.*, 20 Nov. 1981, 643.

[17] Mary Meehan, "Catholic Liberals and Abortion: Time to Move Beyond Agonizing," *Com.*, 20 Nov. 1981, 650–54.

[18] Ibid., 651 (italics Nathanson's). See also Bernard N. Nathanson, *Aborting America* (New York: Doubleday, 1979), 51–52. Nathanson comments: "For their part, of course, the Catholic bishops were to play right into our hands, by their heavy-handed politicking, making abortion appear to be purely a 'Catholic' issue rather than an interreligious one. They also weakened the credibility of the anti-abortion forces because of their unflinching opposition to the major alternatives to abortion: artificial birth control and voluntary sterilization."

[19] Meehan, "Catholic Liberals and Abortion," 654.

[20] James R. Kelly, "Beyond the Stereotypes," *Com.*, 20 Nov. 1981, 654–59.

[21] Peter Steinfels, "The Search for an Alternative: Can Liberal Catholicism Make a Distinct Contribution?" *Com.*, 20 Nov. 1981, 660–64.

[22] "Abortion Ten Years Later," *Com.*, 28 Jan. 1983, 35–37.

[23] On this point, the editorial praised the extraordinary self-critical article by Joyce Evans, respect-life coordinator for the archdiocese of New York ("Prolife Compassion or Crusade?" *America,* 11 Dec. 1982, 373–74). "We know of no similar statement emanating from pro-choice ranks, no self-questioning of that depth, no parallel admission of the limits of one's own position and the humanity of one's adversaries," "Abortion Ten Years Later," 36.

[24] Sidney Callahan and Daniel Callahan, "Breaking Through the Stereotypes: A Surprising Side to the Abortion Debate," *Com.*, 5 Oct. 1984, 520–23.

[25] The list of project participants appears on p. 522. A book resulting from the project was edited by the Callahans, *Abortion: Understanding Differences* (New York: Plenum Press, 1984).

[26] Sidney Callahan, "Abortion and the Sexual Agenda: A Case for Pro-Life Feminism," *Com.*, 25 April 1986, 232–38.

[27] Joan C. Callahan, "The Fetus and Fundamental Rights: Public Policy Requires Compelling Reasons," *Com.*, 11 April 1986, 203–8.

[28] *Com.*, 6 June 1986, 339.

[29] "The Catholic Legacy and Abortion: A Debate," *Com.*, 20 Nov. 1987, 657–80.

[30] "The Editors: Sifting the Arguments," *Com.*, 20 Nov., 1987, 674.

[31] *Com.*, 12 Feb. 1988, 82–87.

Chapter 2

[1] "The Democratic Ticket," *Com.*, 30 July 1976, 483–84.

[2] "The Election," *Com.*, 22 Oct. 1976, 675–76.

[3] "What Carter Forgets," *Com.*, 8 Oct. 1976, 644.

[4] Russell Kirk, "A Vote for Ford," *Com.*, 22 Oct. 1976, 681–83.

[5] Richard J. Neuhaus, "Why I Am For Carter," *Com.*, 22 Oct. 1976, 683–86.

[6] Reed Whittmore, "The Case for McCarthy," *Com.*, 22 Oct. 1976, 686–92; "The Election," ibid., 675.

[7] Whittmore, *Com.*, 22 Oct., 1976, 691.

[8] "The New Union," *Com.*, 19 Nov. 1976, 739–40.

[9] "Political Responsibility: Reflections on an Election Year" (issued 12 Feb. 1976). In *Renewing the Earth: Catholic Documents on Peace, Justice and Liberation*. Edited by David J. O'Brien and Thomas A. Shannon (New York: Doubleday, 1977), 527–37.

[10] Jim Castelli, "How Catholics Voted: Did Carter Really Have a Catholic Problem?" *Com.*, 3 Dec. 1976, 780–82.

[11] "Why Not the Best?" *Com.*, 25 May 1979, 291–92.

[12] "1980—With a Little Help from our Friends," ibid., 292–95.

[13] "'Winning a Nuclear War?'" *Com.*, 28 Mar. 1980, 163–64.

[14] "The Other Contests," *Com.*, 26 Sept. 1980, 515–16.

[15] Thomas E. Cronin, "A Kennedy Delegate in Carter's Camp," *Com.*, 24 Oct. 1980, 586–88.

[16] Michael Novak, "A Switch to Reagan for a Strong America," *Com.*, 24 Oct. 1980, 588–91.

[17] Richard C. Wade, "Throwing My Vote to Anderson," *Com.*, 24 Oct. 1980, 591–93.

[18] "Life After Reagan," *Com.*, 21 Nov. 1980, 643–44.

[19] Jim Castelli, "The Religious Vote," *Com.*, 21 Nov. 1980, 650–51.

[20] "Dr. Reagan's Dubious Medicine," *Com.*, 13 Mar. 1981, 131–32.

[21] "Into El Quagmire," *Com.*, 13 Mar. 1981, 133.

[22] "Race to the Finish," *Com.*, 10 Feb. 1984, 67.

[23] "Mr. Reagan's Civil Religion," *Com.*, 21 Sept. 1984, 483–85.

[24] "A Catholic Woman in the White House?" *Com.*, 10 Aug. 1984, 419–21.

[25] David R. Carlin, "Patchy Garment: How Many Votes Has Bernardin?" *Com.*, 10 Aug., 1984, 422–23.

[26] "Political Responsibility: Choices for the '80s," *Origins* 3, no. 44 (12 April 1984): 732–36.

[27] See Jim Castelli, *A Plea for Common Sense: Resolving the Clash Between Religion and Politics* (San Francisco: Harper and Row, 1988), 82–87.

[28] Joan Barthel, "The Education of a Public Man," *Notre Dame Magazine* 13, no. 5 (Winter 1984–85): 13.

[29] Mario Cuomo, "Religious Belief and Public Morality," *Origins* 14, no. 15 (27 Sept. 1984): 234–240.

[30] "Church and Cuomo," *Com.*, 5 Oct. 1984, 517–18.

[31] See Garry Wills, "A Thoughtful Performance," *Notre Dame Magazine* 13, no. 4 (Autumn 1984): 27.

[32] Richard McBrien, "All the Right Questions," *Notre Dame Magazine* 13, no. 4 (Autumn 1984): 23.

[33] Wills, "A Thoughtful Performance," 27.

[34] Ralph McInerney, "Cuomo Is Wrong," *Notre Dame Magazine* 13, no. 4 (Autumn 1984): 29.

[35] Theodore M. Hesburgh, "A Well-Kept Secret," *Notre Dame Magazine* 13, no. 4 (Autumn 194): 30.

[36] Henry J. Hyde, "The Hardest Case," *Notre Dame Magazine* 13, no. 4 (Autumn 1984): 24.

[37] "Church and Cuomo," 517–18.

[38] Abigail McCarthy, "Cuomo and the Lay Voice: The Concern of '*Commonweal* Catholics,' " *Com.*, 19 Oct. 1984, 550–51.

[39] See Jim Castelli, *A Plea for Common Sense*, 82–87.

[40] Peter Steinfels, "Is Rome Anti-Catholic?" *Com.*, 11 Jan. 1985, 4–5.

[41] "Religion and the '84 Campaign," *Origins* 14, no. 11 (23 Aug. 1984): 161–63; "USCC Says Bishops Non-Partisan," *Origins* 14, no. 19 (25 Oct. 1984): 289–91.

[42] "The Consistent Pro-Life Ethic," *Origins* 14, no. 20 (1 Nov. 1984): 312–13.

[43] "Moral Evaluation and the Spectrum of Life Issues," *Origins* 14, no. 20 (1 Nov. 1984): 311. For Law's response see, ibid., 325.

[44] John J. O'Connor, "Human Lives, Human Rights," *Origins* 14, no. 19 (25 Oct. 1984): 291–301.

[45] Joseph Bernardin, "Religion and Politics: The Future Agenda," *Origins* 14, no. 21 (8 Nov. 1984): 321–28.

[46] See Castelli, *A Plea for Common Sense*, 88–89.

[47] Nancy Amidei, "The Fairness Front: November Was Not Armageddon," *Com.*, 30 Nov. 1984, 645.

[48] Ronald R. Stockton, "No Catholic Women?" *Com.*, 11 Jan. 1985, 28.

[49] John Garvey, "Politics and Religion: Heightened Rhetoric, Deepened Confusion," *Com.*, 2–16 Nov. 1984, 584–85.

[50] Mary C. Segers, "Running Difficulties," *Com.*, 31 Jan. 1986, 54–58.

[51] See Fred Siegel, "The Return to Populism: Democrats Try Harder . . . Again," *Com.*, 22 April 1988, 241–44; Fred Siegel, "Election '88 Competing Elites: The Duke and the Dauphin," *Com.*, 7 Oct. 1988, 523–25; Fred Siegel, "What Liberals Haven't Learned and Why: The Election That Turned Sour," *Com.*, 13 Jan. 1989, 16–20.

[52] Margaret O'Brien Steinfels had become *Commonweal* editor in January 1988.

[53] "Higher Ground," *Com.*, 12 Aug. 1988, 419.

[54] Fred Siegel, "Election '88 Competing Elites: The Duke and the Dauphin," *Com.*, 7 Oct. 1988, 523–25.

[55] "A Door Swings Shut Again," *Com.*, 2 Dec. 1988, 643–44.

[56] David R. Carlin, "Oh, to Be a Hoosier: Why the Democrats Keep Losing," *Com.*, 2 Dec. 1988, 646–47.

[57] Fred Siegel, "What Liberals Haven't Learned and Why," *Com.*, 13 Jan. 1989, 16–20.

[58] "A Door Swings Shut Again," *Com.*, 2 Dec. 1988, 643–44.

Chapter 3

[1] "To Our Readers," *Com.*, 6 Dec. 1974, 229.

[2] John Deedy, "Finis," *Com.*, 15 Sept. 1978, 578.

[3] Interview by the author with Edward S. Skillin, 17 June 1986.

[4] "Staff Changes," *Com.*, 29 Sept. 1978, 612.

[5] Ibid. Steinfels coedited *Death Inside Out* (New York: Harper and Row, 1975) with Robert M. Veach. See also Steinfels's *The Neo-Conservatives: The Men Who Are Changing America's Politics* (New York: Simon and Schuster, 1979).

[6] See Rodger Van Allen, *The Commonweal and American Catholicism*, 173–78.

[7] Interview by author with Peter Steinfels, 17 June 1986.

[8] Peter Steinfels, "Death of a Hero," *Com.*, 7 May 1976, 305.

[9] "John Cogley 1916–76: A Sampler from Two Decades of Writing in *Commonweal*," *Com.*, 7 May 1976, 301–304.

[10] James O'Gara, "In the Thick of It: Honesty, Intellect and Friendship," *Com.*, 28 Mar. 1986, 166–68.

[11] Edward S. Skillin, "George N. Shuster," *Com.*, 18 Feb. 1977, 100–101.

[12] From a private file containing versions of the memo and more substantive responses provided to the author by Peter Steinfels. Hereafter cited as P. Steinfels file.

[13] P. Steinfels file.

[14] P. Steinfels file.

[15] See Van Allen, *The Commonweal and American Catholicism*, 5–7.

[16] P. Steinfels file.

[17] "New Look for a New Era," *Com.*, 27 Oct. 1978, 675–76.

[18] See "Departing Editor," *Com.*, 6 July 1979, 388–89.

[19] "New Editors," *Com.*, 28 Sept. 1979, 517.

[20] "Losing a 'Natural,' " *Com.*, 1 Aug. 1980, 421–22.

[21] "Poetry Editors," *Com.*, 21 Dec. 1979, 709.

[22] James O'Gara, "By Way of Farewell," *Com.*, 23 Mar. 1984, 165–67.

[23] Interview by the author with James O'Gara, 21 Oct. 1986.

[24] See "Dear Jim, 'For the Record,' " *Com.*, 1 June 1984, 324.

[25] "Progress Report," *Com.*, 13 July 1984, 389.

Chapter 4

[1] Letter of Jo McGowan, undated, is in Box 8, File Folder 4 of *The Commonweal* collection in the University of Notre Dame Archives.

[2] Jo McGowan, "Marriage Versus Just Living Together: Acknowledging Life in the Context of Community," *Com.*, 13 Mar. 1981, 142–44.

[3] See *Com.*, 12 Mar. 1982, 154.

[4] Robert Phillips, "On Being Flannery O'Connor," *Com.*, 13 April 1979, 216–20.

[5] Ibid., 219.

[6] Ibid., 217. See also *Letters of Flannery O'Connor: The Habit of Being*, ed. Sally Fitzgerald (New York: Farrar, Straus and Giroux, 1979), 258.

[7] Frances Taliaferro, *Harper's*, April 1978, 84. Biographical material from the interview with Mary Gordon in Frances C. Locher, ed., *Contemporary Authors,* Vol. 102, 224. *Commonweal* published a mixed review of *Final Payments* (see James M. Rawley and Robert F. Moss, "The Pulp of the Matter: From Melodrama to Catholic Fiction," *Com.*, 27 Oct. 1978, 685–89) and a highly praising review of *The Company of Women* (see Sally Fitzgerald, "Harsh Love and Human Happiness," *Com.*, 19 June 1981, 375–77). See also Diana Cooper-Clark, "An Interview with Mary Gordon," *Com.*, 9 May 1980, 270–73.

[8] Mary Gordon, "Coming to Terms with Mary," *Com.*, 15 Jan. 1982, 11–14.

[9] Rosemary Booth, "A Concentration of Purpose: The Artistic Journey of Mary Gordon," *Com.*, 12 Aug. 1988, 426–30.

[10] Kenneth L. Woodward, "Gays in the Clergy," *Newsweek,* 23 Feb. 1987, 58–60.

[11] "The Homosexual and the Church" and two articles by Tom F. Driver and Peter E. Fink, in *Com.*, 6 April 1973; discussion, 1 June 1973, 311–13. See also Elred and Bernardin in *Com.*, 26 Dec. 1986, 680–84.

[12] Richard McBrien, "Homosexuality and the Priesthood: Questions We Can't Keep in the Closet," *Com.*, 19 June 1987, 380–83.

[13] "An Exchange of Views: Homosexuality and the Priesthood," *Com.*, 11 Sept. 1987, 493–97.

[14] Dean R. Hoge, *The Future of Catholic Leadership: Responses to the Priest Shortage* (Kansas City, Mo.: Sheed and Ward, 1987).

[15] John Garvey, *Saints for Confused Times* (Chicago: Thomas More, 1986). Some other books written or edited by Garvey include *The Ways We Are Together: Reflections on Marriage, Family and Sexuality* (Chicago: Thomas More, 1983); *Modern Spirituality: An Anthology* (Springfield, Ill.: Templegate, 1985); and *Henri Nouwen* (Springfield, Ill.: Templegate, 1988).

[16] John Garvey, "A Married Layman on Celibacy," *Com.*, 26 Oct. 1979, 585–88.

[17] Robert Imbelli, "Correspondence," *Com.*, 7 Dec. 1979, 674.

[18] John Garvey, "Church Beyond Church," *Com.*, 21 Nov. 1980, 646–47.

[19] John Garvey, "Lord Acton, Power and Papal Infallibility," *Com.*, 1 Feb. 1980, 42–44.

[20] John Garvey, "Family Photographs," *Com.*, 22 April 1988, 233–34.

[21] John Garvey, "Man Becomes God: A Hard Saying at Christmastime," *Com.*, 23 Dec. 1977, 815–18.

[22] John Tracy Ellis, "Garvey Excels Garvey," *Com.*, 25 Jan. 1985, 34.

[23] John Garvey, "Religion and Reflex," *Com.*, 1 June 1984, 327–28.

[24] Abigail McCarthy, *Private Faces/Public Places* (New York: Doubleday, 1972), 435.

[25] Abigail McCarthy, "Don't Call Us, We'll Call You: What the Synod Said to Women," *Com.*, 4 Dec. 1987, 695–96.

[26] Abigail McCarthy, "Justice for Mothers: Reflections for the Annual Spring Ritual," *Com.*, 23 May 1980, 297–98.

[27] Abigail McCarthy, "The Ideal and the Issue: Facing Reality in Helping Families," *Com.*, 25 April 1980, 232–33.

[28] Abigail McCarthy, "The Spirit of Venantia: What Sister Really Said," *Com.*, 25 Sept. 1982, 487–488.

[29] See *Origins* 13, no. 8 (7 July 1983): 129–42, for both of these documents.

[30] Abigail McCarthy, "The Nuns' (Old) Story: Encountering Obstacles Is Nothing New," *Com.*, 18 Nov. 1983, 616–17.

Chapter 5

[1] Raymond Schroth, "Why the Pope Should Resign," *Com.*, 11 Nov. 1977, 707–8. This editorial was written by associate editor Raymond Schroth, S. J. See Box 21, *Commonweal* collection in the University of Notre Dame Archives. In standard *Commonweal* practice, the editorial was approved by the then editors, James O'Gara and John Deedy.

[2] John Jay Hughes, "Lessons After John Paul I," *Com.*, 13 Oct. 1978, 644–45. For editorial comment on the death of Pope Paul VI, see *Com.*, 18 Aug. 1978, 515–16 and "Correspondence," 610.

[3] Peter Hebblethwaite, *The Year of Three Popes* (New York: Collins, 1978), 153.

[4] Ibid., 154.

[5] John Jay Hughes, "A New Era: Exorcising the Demons of History," *Com.*, 10 Nov. 1978, 708–10.

[6] John Tracy Ellis, "The Historian's Eye," *Com.*, 22 Dec. 1978, 802.

[7] "The Worlds of John Paul II," *Com.*, 10 Nov. 1978, 707–8.

[8] "From Charisma to Leadership," *Com.*, 26 Oct. 1979, 579–80.

[9] Peter Hebblethwaite, *The New Inquisition?* (New York: Harper and Row, 1978), 9.

[10] "Who's Disturbing the Faithful?" *Com.*, 1 Feb. 1980, 37–38.

[11] Hebblethwaite, *The New Inquisition?*, 105.

[12] "Polarization in the Church?" *Com.*, 18 May 1984, 291–93.

[13] Albert Outler, "Chill in the Church," *Com.*, 21 Sept. 1984, 482.

[14] Stanley Hauerwas and Robert Wilken, "Protestants and the Pope: John Paul II and Christian Unity," *Com.*, 15 Feb. 1980, 80–85. J. M. R. Tillard, *The Bishop of Rome* (Wilmington, Del.: Michael Glazier, 1983), 58–59.

[15] Richard John Neuhaus, The Catholic Moment: *The Paradox of the Church in the Postmodern World* (San Francisco: Harper and Row, 1987), *x*, 161–233, and 284. In 1990, Neuhaus himself became a Roman Catholic.

[16] "Heart and Mind," *Com.*, 5 June 1981, 324–25.

[17] "On the Pope's Gesture," *Com.*, 10 Feb. 1984, 68–69.

[18] Interview by author with Peter Steinfels, 17 June 1986.

[19] "What's in a Name?" *Com.*, 25 Sept. 1987, 515–16.

Chapter 6

[1] Interview with Peter Steinfels, 17 June 1986.

[2] One of the many places in which the document has been published is John Tracy Ellis, ed., *Documents of American Catholic History*, vol. 3 (Wilmington, Del.: Michael Glazier, 1987), 776–887.

[3] Ibid., 776.

[4] For a complete list see *Origins* 12, no. 20 (28 Oct. 1982): 326.

[5] James Reston, *New York Times*, 20 Oct. 1985; George F. Kennan, *New York Times*, 1 May 1983; both as quoted in Ellis*, Documents of American Catholic History*, 776–77.

[6] "The Bishops and the Bomb: Nine Responses," *Com.*, 13 Aug. 1982, 424–40. The respondents were John Langan, William V. Shannon, Joan Chittester, Philip Odeen, Thomas J. Downey, James Finn, Gordon C. Zahn, William J. Nagle, and Charles E. Curran.

[7] "A Milestone for the Bishops," *Com.*, 3 Dec. 1982, 644. The quote, which was incorporated into the document, is from John Paul II's address to the United Nations Special Session on Disarmament.

[8] See the sections on Vietnam and World War II in Van Allen, *The Commonweal and American Catholicism*.

[9] "Is Deterrence Moral?" *Com.*, 8 May 1987, 259–61; and "An Editorial Dissent," *Com.*, 22 May 1987, 309–10.

[10] "A Milestone for the Bishops," 644.

[11] "Time to Accept the Challenge," *Com.*, 6 May 1983, 259–60.

[12] *Challenge of Peace*, Paragraph 147, in John Tracy Ellis, ed., *Documents of American Catholic History*, Vol. 3 (Wilmington, Del.: Michael Glazier, 1987), 831.

[13] Gerald P. Fogarty, "Why the Pastoral Is Shocking: Not Afraid to Challenge Government Policy," *Com.*, 3 June 1983, 335–38.

Chapter 7

[1] Peter Steinfels, "Michael Novak and His Ultrasuper Democraticapitalism," *Com.*, 14 Jan. 1983, 11–16.

[2] Michael Novak, *Confession of a Catholic* (San Francisco: Harper and Row, 1983), 12–13.

[3] Ralph McInerny, "Cinque Anni Fa," *Crisis* (Nov. 1987): 6–7.

[4] Interview by author with Ralph McInerny, 13 Jan. 1988.

[5] Michael Novak, "Moral Clarity in a Nuclear Age," *Catholicism in Crisis* 1, no. 4 (March 1983), and *National Review* (1 April 1983).

[6] McInerny, "Cinque," 7.

[7] Ibid.

[8] Michael Novak, "Frequent Even Daily Communion," in *The Catholic Case for Contraception*, Daniel J. Callahan, ed. (New York: Doubleday, 1969), 92–102.

[9] Michael Novak, "Rome, Spur of Intellectual Freedom," *Crisis* 7, no. 6 (June 1989): 45.

[10] Peter Steinfels, "Michael Novak and His Ultrasuper Democraticapitalism," 16.

[11] Michael Novak, *The Spirit of Democratic Capitalism* (New York: Simon and Schuster, 1982), 171–82.

[12] Daniel Bell, *The Cultural Contradictions of Capitalism*, as quoted in Peter Steinfels, "Does Capitalism, Equal Pluralism, Equal Democracy?" *Com.*, 11 Feb. 1983, 79–85.

[13] Peter Steinfels, ibid., 84.

[14] Peter Steinfels, ibid., 83.

[15] Bernard Murchland, Mary Ash, Robert Benne, Michael Novak, and Peter Steinfels, "Correspondence," *Com.*, 17 June 1983, 354, 376–82.

[16] Ibid., 377.

[17] Peter Steinfels, "Michael Novak and His Ultrasuper Democraticapitalism," 11.

[18] Bernard Murchland and Peter Steinfels, "Correspondence," ibid., 354 and 381.

[19] Charles Krauthammer, "The Two Conservatisms," *New Republic* (16 June 1982): 26–30.

[20] James Hitchcock, "Fire Bells in the Night," *National Review* (23 July 1982): 905–6.

[21] Michael J. Kerlin, "Finality Is Not the Language of Politics," *America* (23 Oct. 1982): 236–37.

[22] Michael Novak, "Correspondence," *Com.*, 17 June 1983, 378.

[23] Peter Steinfels, ibid., 381.

[24] This did not mean, of course, that the debate had been resolved.

[25] For the complete list see "Economic Justice for All: Catholic Social Teaching and the U.S. Economy," *Origins* 16, no. 24 (27 Nov. 1986): 454–55.

[26] *Origins* 14, nos. 22/23 (15 Nov. 1984): 337–83.

[27] Reprinted in *Catholicism in Crisis* 2, no. 12 (Nov. 1984): 1–54.

[28] Steve Askin, "Rightist Catholics Pounce Before Hierarchy Speaks," *National Catholic Reporter*, vol. 30 (Nov. 1984): 1.

[29] "Shortchanging the Pastoral," *Com.*, 30 Nov. 1984, 643–44.

[30] For Novak, Finn, and the editors' comments, see "Correspondence," *Com.*, 8 Feb. 1985, 66, 94.

[31] "Shortchanging the Pastoral," ibid.

[32] *Com.*, 30 Nov. 1984, 650–54: Paul Steidl-Meier, "A Reformist Document"; F. Byron Nahser, "A Needed Third Question"; Rachel A. Willis, "For a Democratic Economy"; and Rudy Oswald, "Labor and the Bishops' Letter."

[33] Michael Harrington, "The Future of Poverty," *Com.*, 2–16 Nov. 1984, 625–32.

[34] "Revising the Letter," *Com.*, 8 March 1985, 132–34.

[35] "The Search for a Just Economy," *Com.*, 5 Dec. 1986, 643–44.

[36] Rembert Weakland, "The Economics Pastoral and the Signs of the Times," *Origins* 14, no. 24 (29 Nov. 1984): 395.

[37] "The Search for a Just Economy," ibid., 644.

[38] Par. 17, "A Pastoral Message," *Economic Justice for All.*

[39] "The Search for a Just Economy," ibid.

[40] For example, see the series of articles beginning with Robert N. Bellah, "Resurrecting the Common Good," *Com.*, 18 Dec. 1987, 735–41.

Chapter 8

[1] As quoted in "The Synod: Hope and Apprehension," *Com.*, 8 Feb. 1985, 67.

[2] Ibid.

[3] Ibid.

[4] As quoted by Avery Dulles, "Authority: The Divided Legacy," *Com.*, 12 July 1985, 400–403. See Walter M. Abbott, ed., *The Documents of Vatican II* (New York: Herder and Herder, 1966), 677.

[5] See Abbott, ibid., paragraph 25 of "Dogmatic Constitution on the Church," 47–50, which Dulles cites parenthetically.

[6] Dulles, "Authority: The Divided Legacy," ibid.

[7] Elisabeth Schussler Fiorenza, "The Discipleship of Equals," *Com.*, 9 Aug. 1985, 432–37.

[8] See Abbott, *The Documents of Vatican II*, ibid., paragraph 9 of "Decree on the Apostolate of the Laity," 500, which Fiorenza cites parenthetically.

[9] See Abbott, ibid., paragraph 29 of "Pastoral Constitution on the Church in the Modern World," 227–28, which Fiorenza cites parenthetically.

[10] See Abbott, ibid., paragraph 32 of "Dogmatic Constitution on the Church," 58–59, which Fiorenza cites parenthetically.

[11] See David J. O'Brien and Thomas A. Shannon, eds., *Catholic Social Thought: The Documentary Heritage* (Maryknoll, N. Y.: Orbis, 1992), paragraph 40 of "Justice in the World," 295.

[12] Fiorenza's *In Memory of Her: A Feminist Theological Reconstruction of Christian Origins* (New York: Crossroad, 1983), was a significant scholarly work supporting these contentions.

[13] See Abbott, *The Documents of Vatican II*, ibid., paragraph 42 of "Pastoral Constitution on the Church in the Modern World" (241–42), which Fiorenza cites parenthetically.

[14] Ibid., Elisabeth Schussler Fiorenza, "The Discipleship of Equals."

[15] The other articles were Gregory Baum, "After Liberal Optimism, What?" *Com.*, 21 June 1985, 363–67; Joseph A. Komonchak, "What's Happening to Doctrine?" *Com.*, 6 Sept. 1985, 456–59; Lisa Sowle Cahill, "Morality: The Deepening Crisis," *Com.*, 20 Sept. 1985, 496–99; and Bernard F. Swain, "Spirituality in Ferment," *Com.*, 4 Oct. 1985, 521–25.

[16] "From the Council to the Synod," *Com.*, 18 Oct. 1985, 559–81. The participants were Raymond Flynn, Mary Durkin, Jack Miles, Peter Quinn, Barbara Grizzuti Harrison, J. Peter Grace, Tom Fox, Wilfrid Sheed, Mary Gordon, Marilyn Chapin Massey, Jean Vanier, Eugene McCarthy, Juli Loesch, Camille D'Arienzo, Keith C. Burris, Mary Pat Kelly, Palma E. Formica, Stuart Dybek, Nancy Rambusch, Joseph Sobran, and Garry Wills.

[17] Garry Willis, ibid., 580.

[18] J. Peter Grace, ibid., 566–67.

[19] Barbara Grizzuti Harrison, ibid., 565.

[20] Joseph Sobran, ibid., 580–81.

[21] Mary Durkin, ibid., 560–61.

[22] Raymond Flynn, ibid., 559–60.

[23] Wilfrid Sheed, ibid., 568–69.

[24] Tom Fox, ibid., 567–68.

[25] Camille D'Arienzo, ibid., 574–75.

[26] Nancy Rambusch, ibid., 579–80.

[27] Palma E. Formica, ibid., 577–78.

[28] Jean Vanier, ibid., 570–71.

[29] Tom Fox, ibid., 567–68.

[30] Peter Quinn, ibid., 564–65.

[31] Clare Huchet-Bishop, "Distressing Lacuna," *Com.*, 20 Dec. 1985, 690.

[32] Harvey Cox, "Closing the Windows?" *Com.*, 20 Dec., 1985, 711.

[33] Peter Steinfels, "So Far, So Good, So What: Conflicts and Code Words: A Sober Look at the Synod," ibid., 698–700.

[34] Paul Surlis, "Laying Claim: The Synod Must Define Itself," *Com.*, 15 Nov. 1985, 629.

[35] Elisabeth Schussler Fiorenza, "So Far, So Bad," *Com.*, 31 Jan. 1986, 44–46.

[36] Eugene McCarthy, "From the Council to the Synod," *Com.*, 18 Oct. 1985, 572.

[37] Tom Fox, ibid., 568.

Chapter 9

[1] Peter Steinfels, "Dear Friend of *Commonweal*" letter, May 1986.

[2] Interview by author with Edward Skillin, 17 June 1986.

[3] Peter Steinfels, letter, "Dear Friend of *Commonweal*," May 1986.

[4] From the file of responses in *Commonweal*'s New York office.

[5] "The New Look," *Com.*, 16 Jan. 1987, 4–5.

[6] "The *Commonweal* White Paper," *Com.*, 2 June 1989, 324.

[7] Emil Antonucci, "Our Task Is to Create Worlds: An Artist and the Experience of God," *Com.*, 2 June 1989, 334–35.

[8] For more detail, see Van Allen, *The Commonweal and American Catholicism*, 76–77; also *Com.*, 1 April 1938, 620.

[9] "A Change of Editors," *Com.*, 4 Dec. 1987, 693. Margaret O'Brien Steinfels's remarks, *Commonweal Associates Newsletter* (Winter 1988) and interview with the author, 20 Oct. 1989.

[10] "A Change of Editors," ibid.

[11] Michael Williams, "An Open Letter to the Editors of *The Commonweal*," *Com.*, 17 Aug. 1945, 428–30.

[12] Interview with James O'Gara, 21 Oct. 1986. O'Gara said *Commonweal* "had less women than we would have liked."

[13] See Van Allen, *The Commonweal and American Catholicism*, 36.

[14] *Commonweal*'s other regular columnists were John Garvey, J. Bryan Hehir, and David R. Carlin, Jr.

[15] Letter from Anne Robertson to the author, 13 Aug. 1986.

[16] Text of eulogy supplied to the author by Margaret O'Brien Steinfels. See also "Remembering Anne," *Com.*, 8 Sept. 1989, 452–53.

[17] Edward S. Skillin, "In Memoriam, Kathleen Casey Craig," *Com.*, 13 Jan. 1989, 6. See also Van Allen, *The Commonweal and American Catholicism*, 124.

Chapter 10

[1] See "Manipulating Death," "Getting the Point," and "The Twenty Million," *Com.*, 15 Jan. 1988, 3–5.

[2] See "Time to Do Right," "Time to Move," and "Maintaining Perspective," *Com.*, 29 Jan. 1988, 33–38.

[3] "A Resourceful 17 Years," *Com.*, 29 Jan. 1988, 38.

[4] "Partners in the Mystery of Redemption: A Pastoral Response to Women's Concerns for Church and Society," *Origins* 17, no. 45 (21 April 1988): 757–88.

[5] "Dear John," *Com.*, 22 April 1988, 227–28.

[6] Abigail McCarthy, "Impossible Twenty Years Ago," *Com.*, 3 June 1988, 326–27. The editorial stated: "A decade ago this pastoral could not have been written."

7 "Sexism, Sin and Grace: Responses to the Bishops' Letter," *Com.*, 17 June 1988, 361–66. The respondents were Jane Redmont, Marylee Mitcham, Mary C. Segers, Emilie Griffin, Jean Bethke Elshtain, and Anne E. Patrick.

8 Ed Marciniak, "Women Only?" *Com.*, 12 Aug. 1988, 418.

9 "Anniversary Waltz," *Com.*, 15 July 1988, 387–88.

10 Ibid.

11 Greg Burke, "Meeting Praises the Wisdom of *Humanae Vitae* Message," *National Catholic Register,* vol. LXIV, no. 34 (21 Aug. 1988): 1, 8.

12 John C. Cort, "A Dissenter Recants," *Com.*, 23 Sept. 1988, 482, 505–6.

13 Frank C. Arricale, "Felix Culpa," *Com.*, 23 Sept. 1988, 482.

14 "The Editors Reply," *Com.*, 23 Sept. 1988, 510–11.

15 Bernard Haring, "Does God Condemn Contraception? A Question for the Whole Church," *Com.*, 10 Feb. 1989, 69–71.

16 "The Cologne Declaration: Authority Out of Bounds," *Com.*, 24 Feb. 1989, 102–4.

17 See "Decree on Ecumenism," paragraph 11 in Walter Abbott, ed. *The Documents of Vatican II,* ibid., 354.

18 "The Cologne Declaration: Authority Out of Bounds," ibid., 103.

19 Haring, "Does God Condemn Contraception?," 70.

20 Edward S. Skillin, Letter to *Commonweal* Associates, 10 June 1989.

21 Margaret O'Brien Steinfels, "The Church and Its Public Life," *America* (10 June 1989): 550–58.

22 See "Pastoral Constitution on the Church in the Modern World," paragraph 1 in Walter Abbott, ed. *The Documents of Vatican II,* 199.

[23] See "Declaration on Religious Freedom," paragraph 12 in Abbott, ibid., 692–93.

[24] Margaret O'Brien Steinfels, "The Church and Its Public Life," ibid., 550–58.

Chapter 11

[1] J. Bryan Hehir, "East-West, North-South: Breaking the 'Logic of the Blocs,' " *Com.*, 17 Nov. 1989, 614–15.

[2] "Consider the Wall," *Com.*, 1 Dec. 1989, 659–60.

[3] Czarina Wilpert, "Euphoria and Beyond: New Immigrants and Old," *Com.*, 15 Dec. 1989, 695–97.

[4] Edward K. Braxton, "Loaded Terms: What's in a Name?" *Com.*, 2 June 1989, 328–29.

[5] Tom O'Brien, "Facts of (Ghetto) Life," *Com.*, 14 July 1989, 402–3.

[6] Bridget Balthrop Morton, "Daniel: Beloved By God and By Me," *Com.*, 20 Oct. 1989, 562–63.

[7] Francis C. Skilling, "About Malcolm X," *Com.*, 15 Dec. 1989, 690.

[8] "Too Many Abortions," *Com.*, 11 Aug. 1989, 419–20.

[9] "Abortion: What Does 'Webster' Mean?" *Com.*, 11 Aug. 1989, 425–28. Other participants were Sidney Callahan, Mary C. Segers, E. J. Dionne, Juli Loesch Wiley, Annie Lally Milhaven, and Burke J. Balch.

[10] Margaret O'Brien Steinfels, "The Politics of Evasion," *Com.*, 3 Nov. 1989, 579–80.

[11] "Strategy Time," *Com.*, 26 Jan. 1990, 36.

[12] "Strategy Time II," *Com.*, 9 Feb. 1990, 68–69.

[13] Mario M. Cuomo, "Joining the Debate," *Com.*, 23 March 1990, 170, 196–99.

[14] "By Way of Reply," *Com.*, 6 April 1990, 203–4.

Chapter 12

[1] Edward S. Skillin, "A Goodly Company," *Com.*, 17 Nov. 1989, 613.

[2] David J. O'Brien, "Join It, Work It, Fight It: American Catholics and the American Way," *Com.*, 17 Nov. 1989, 624–30.

[3] Albert Raboteau, "Preaching the Word and Doing It: Black Catholics in America," *Com.*, 17 Nov. 1989, 631–35.

[4] Sidney Callahan, "Getting Our Heads Together: An Agenda for Catholic Intellectuals," *Com.*, 17 Nov. 1989, 635–42.

[5] Susan Cahill, John Deedy, Andrew M. Greeley, Monika K. Hellwig, Theresa Kane, Abigail McCarthy, John J. O'Connor, William K. Reilly, Peggy Rosenthal, George Weigel, and Kenneth L. Woodward, "Challenges Facing U.S. Catholics: The Next Ten Years," *Com.*, 17 Nov. 1989, 617–23.

[6] Ibid., 620.

[7] Ibid., 618.

[8] Ibid., 622.

[9] Ibid., 620–21.

[10] See John F.X. Harriott, "My Fears for the Church," *The Tablet*, 23 Sept. 1989, 1078.

[11] "Onward," *Com.*, 17 Nov. 1989, 611–12.

Conclusions: A Very Worthy Conversation

[1] Margaret O'Brien Steinfels, "Beyond Assimilation: Let's Get Wise," in *The Catholic Church and American Culture: Reciprocity and Challenge*, ed. Cassian Yuhaus (Mahwah, N.J.: Paulist Press, 1990), 24–36.

[2] See *Com.*, 20 Nov. 1987, 657–80. In 1984, Justus George Lawler recorded a complaint that "the fact that one of our most distin-

guished and compassionate moralists, Daniel Maguire, cannot find a forum in journals such as *Commonweal* seems to me indicative of the rigidity of Catholic opinion in the eighties in contrast to its flexibility in the sixties." "The *Continuum* Generation," *U. S. Catholic Historian* 4, no. 1 (1984): 82. Editor Peter Steinfels recalls that Maguire called at a time *Commonweal* was running a Mary Meehan article with other responses, and Maguire wanted to do a piece on how the bishops handled abortion. He was given a chance to compose a two thousand-word response to Meehan. He wanted four thousand words or nothing. Eventually his piece appeared in the *Christian Century*. Interview by author with Peter Steinfels, 30 July 1986.

[3] *Com.,* 8 Dec. 1978, 771–73.

[4] "Strategy Time III," *Com.*, 23 Feb. 1990, 99–101. See Schlesinger, *New York Times*, 2 Feb. 1990.

[5] "Challenges Facing U.S. Catholics: The Next Ten Years," *Com.*, 17 Nov. 1989, 617–23.

[6] "From the Council to the Synod," *Com.*, 18 Oct. 1985, 559–81.

[7] See Section IX of "From The Council to the Synod."

[8] See *Commonweal Associates Newsletter*, June 1983.

[9] Ibid.

[10] *Com.,* 14 Jan. 1983, 11–16.

[11] "Correspondence," *Com.*, 17 June 1983, 354.

[12] "On the Pope's Gesture," *Com.*, 10 Feb. 1984, 68.

[13] Margaret O'Brien Steinfels, "Beyond Assimilation: Let's Get Wise," 35.

[14] Ibid., 36.

[15] See Van Allen, *The Commonweal and American Catholicism*, 12–14.

[16] *Com.,* 17 Nov. 1989, 624–630.

[17] See Herve Carrier, *Gospel Message and Human Cultures* (Pittsburgh: Duquesne University Press, 1989), 165.

[18] Guilday quotes from letters to Lawrason Riggs, James J. Walsh, and John J. Wynne, as found in David J. O'Brien, "Peter Guilday: The Catholic Intellectual in the Post-Modernist Church," in *Studies in Catholic History*, ed. Nelson H. Minnick, Robert B. Eno, and Robert F. Trisco (Wilmington, Del.: Michael Glazier, 1985), 260–306.

[19] John Garvey, "The Importance of *Commonweal*," *Notre Dame Magazine* 11, no. 3 (July 1982): 35–38.

[20] George Weigel, *Com.*, 17 Nov. 1989, 621.

[21] Arij Roest Crollius, *What Is So New about Inculturation?* (Rome: Pontifical Gregorian University, 1984), 14. This volume is number five in the series *Inculturation: Working Papers in Living Faith and Cultures*, edited by Arij Roest Crollius, published by the Centre "Cultures and Religions" at the Pontifical Gregorian University. See also, Rodger Van Allen "Catholicism in the United States: Some Elements of Creative Inculturation" in *Creative Inculturation and the Unity of Faith*, ed. Arij Roest Crollius (Rome: Pontifical Gregorian University, 1986), 55–76.

[22] John Cogley, "The Catholic and the Liberal Society," America CI (4 July 1959): 495. This passage is frequently quoted by David J. O'Brien. See *The Renewal of American Catholicism* (New York: Paulist Press, 1972), 8.

[23] Gerald P. Fogarty, *The Vatican and the American Hierarchy 1870–1965* (Wilmington, Del.: Michael Glazier, 1985), 190–93.

[24] Van Allen, *The Commonweal and American Catholicism*, 194.

Afterword

[1] As quoted in *Commonweal Associates Newsletter*, Spring 1988. See Van Allen, *The Commonweal and American Catholicism* for information on Skillin's earlier years with *Commonweal*.

² See *Commonweal Associates Newsletter*, Spring 1988.

³ Ibid.

⁴ Based on several hours of interviews by the author with Skillin and other *Commonweal* editors.

⁵ *Commonweal Associates Newsletter*, Spring 1988.

Bibliography

Abbott, Walter M., ed. *The Documents of Vatican II.* New York: Herder and Herder, 1966.

Bell, Daniel. *The Cultural Contradictions of Capitalism.* New York: Basic Books, 1976.

Benne, Robert. *The Ethic of Democratic Capitalism.* Philadelphia: Fortress, 1981.

Callahan, Sidney, and Daniel Callahan. *Abortion: Understanding Differences.* New York: Plenum Press, 1984.

Carrier, Herve. *Gospel Message and Human Cultures.* Pittsburgh: Duquesne University Press, 1989.

Castelli, Jim. *A Plea for Common Sense: Resolving the Clash Between Religion and Politics.* San Francisco: Harper and Row, 1988.

Cogley, John. *Catholic America.* 1973. Expanded and updated by Rodger Van Allen. Kansas City, Mo.: Sheed and Ward, 1986.

Crollius, Arij Roest, ed. *What Is So New about Inculturation?* Vol. 5 of *Inculturation: Working Papers in Living Faith and Cultures.* Rome: Pontifical Gregorian University, 1984.

————, ed. *Creative Inculturation and the Unity of Faith.* Vol. 8 of *Inculturation: Working Papers in Living Faith and Cultures.* Rome: Pontifical Gregorian University, 1986.

Ellis, John Tracy, ed. *Documents of American Catholic History* Vol. 3. Wilmington, Del.: Michael Glazier, 1987.

Ferraro, Geraldine. *Ferraro, My Story.* New York: Bantam, 1985.

Fiorenza, Elisabeth Schussler. *In Memory of Her: A Feminist Theological Reconstruction of Christian Origins.* New York: Crossroad, 1983.

Fitzgerald, Sally, ed. *Letters of Flannery O'Connor: The Habit of Being.* New York: Farrar, Straus and Giroux, 1979.

Fogarty, Gerald P. *The Vatican and the American Hierarchy 1870–1965.* Wilmington, Del.: Michael Glazier, 1985.

Garvey, John. *The Ways We Are Together: Reflections on Marriage, Family and Sexuality.* Chicago: Thomas More, 1983.

————, ed. *Modern Spirituality: An Anthology.* Springfield, Ill.: Templegate, 1985.

————. *Saints for Confused Times.* Chicago: Thomas More, 1986.

————. *Henri Nouwen.* Springfield, Ill.: Templegate, 1988.

Glendon, Mary Ann. *Abortion and Divorce in Western Law.* Cambridge, Mass.: Harvard University Press, 1987.

Greeley, Andrew M., and Mary Greeley Durkin. *A Church to Come Home to.* Chicago: Thomas More, 1982.

————. *Angry Catholic Women.* Chicago: Thomas More, 1984.

————. *How to Save the Catholic Church.* New York: Viking, 1984.

Greeley, Andrew M., and Peter H. Rossi. *The Education of Catholic Americans.* Chicago: Aldine Publishing, 1966.

Hebblethwaite, Peter. *The New Inquisition?* New York: Harper and Row, 1978.

————. *The Year of Three Popes.* New York: Collins, 1978.

Hoge, Dean R. *The Future of Catholic Leadership: Responses to the Priest Shortage.* Kansas City, Mo.: Sheed and Ward, 1987.

McCarthy, Abigail. *Private Faces/Public Places.* New York: Doubleday, 1972.

Minnick, Nelson H., Robert B. Eno, and Robert F. Trisco, eds. *Studies in Catholic History.* Wilmington, Del.: Michael Glazier, 1985.

Nathanson, Bernard N. *Aborting America*. New York: Doubleday, 1979.

Neuhaus, Richard John. *The Catholic Moment: The Paradox of the Church in the Postmodern World*. San Francisco: Harper and Row, 1987.

Novak, Michael. *The Open Church*. New York: Macmillan, 1964.

————. *A Theology for Radical Politics*. New York: Herder and Herder, 1969.

————. *The Rise of the Unmeltable Ethnics*. New York: Macmillan, 1972.

————. *The Spirit of Democratic Capitalism*. New York: Simon and Schuster, 1982.

————. *Confession of a Catholic*. San Francisco: Harper and Row, 1983.

O'Brien, David J. *The Renewal of American Catholicism*. New York: Paulist Press, 1972.

O'Brien, David J., and Thomas A. Shannon, eds. *Renewing the Earth: Catholic Documents on Peace, Justice and Liberation*. New York: Doubleday, 1977.

————, eds. *Catholic Social Thought: The Documentary Heritage*. Maryknoll, N.Y.: Orbis, 1992.

Siegel, Fred. *Troubled Journey: From Pearl Harbor to Ronald Reagan*. New York: Hill and Wang, 1984.

Steinfels, Peter. *The Neo-Conservatives: The Men Who Are Changing America's Politics*. New York: Simon and Schuster, 1979.

Steinfels, Peter, and Robert M. Veach. *Death Inside Out*. New York: Harper and Row, 1975.

Tillard, J. M. R. *The Bishop of Rome*. Wilmington, Del.: Michael Glazier, 1983.

Van Allen, Rodger. *The Commonweal and American Catholicism.* Philadelphia: Fortress, 1974.

Yuhaus, Cassian, ed. *The Catholic Church and American Culture: Reciprocity and Challenge.* Mahwah, N. J.: Paulist Press, 1990.

Index